TABE
Practice Questions

TABE Practice Tests & Review for the
Test of Adult Basic Education

Dear Future Exam Success Story:

First of all, **THANK YOU** for purchasing Mometrix study materials!

Second, congratulations! You are one of the few determined test-takers who are committed to doing whatever it takes to excel on your exam. **You have come to the right place.** We developed these practice tests with one goal in mind: to deliver you the best possible approximation of the questions you will see on test day.

Standardized testing is one of the biggest obstacles on your road to success, which only increases the importance of doing well in the high-pressure, high-stakes environment of test day. Your results on this test could have a significant impact on your future, and these practice tests will give you the repetitions you need to build your familiarity and confidence with the test content and format to help you achieve your full potential on test day.

Your success is our success

We would love to hear from you! If you would like to share the story of your exam success or if you have any questions or comments in regard to our products, please contact us at **800-673-8175** or **support@mometrix.com**.

Thanks again for your business and we wish you continued success!

Sincerely,
The Mometrix Test Preparation Team

TABLE OF CONTENTS

Practice Test #1

Language Practice Questions

For Questions 1-3, select the correct punctuation mark for the sentence.

1. Historians generally believe that the tulip was introduced into Europe. When the Holy Roman Emperor Ferdinand I acquired the bulbs in Turkey and sent them to a Flemish botanist named Charles de l'Ecluse.

    A. ,
    B. ;
    C. :
    D. None

2. The popularity of the tulip immediately spread and developed into what became known as "Tulip Mania" in the Netherlands.

    A. .
    B. ,
    C. :
    D. None

3. The solid-colored tulips started the craze but it was the multicolored tulips that were most popular and brought the most money.

    A. ;
    B. ,
    C. .
    D. None

For Questions 4-6, choose the best word or phrase to complete the sentence.

4. Is the new student coming out to lunch with ____?

    A. we
    B. our
    C. us
    D. they

5. ___ picking up groceries one of the things you are supposed to do?

    A. Is
    B. Am
    C. Is it
    D. Are

6. ____ screaming took the shopkeeper by surprise.

    A. We
    B. They
    C. Them
    D. Our

For Questions 7-17, identify the sentence that contains an error in usage, punctuation or grammar. If there are no errors, choose answer choice "D."

7.

    A. Fear of the number thirteen is called "triskaidekaphobia."
    B. The earwig's name originates in the myth that the insect burrows into the human ear to lay its eggs.
    C. The longest word recorded in an English dictionary are "Pneumonoultramicroscopicsilicovolcanokoniosis."
    D. No mistake.

8.

    A. "Stewardesses," "desegregated," and "reverberated" are the longest words a person can type using only his or her left hand.
    B. The largest catfish ever catch is 646 pounds, the size of an adult brown bear.
    C. A flyswatter has holes in it to reduce air resistance.
    D. No mistake.

9.

    A. The canoe cut a clear swath through the algae.
    B. Though widely ridiculed when first proposed, Alfred Wegener's theory of plate tectonics is now an accepted explanation of how continents are formed.
    C. Though a highly influentially anthropologist, Claude Levi-Strauss often took criticism for spending little time in the field studying real cultures.
    D. No mistake.

10.

    A. Fiction writer David Foster Wallace, author of the influential novel *Infinite Jest*, also authored a book surveying all of the significant theories of infinity in the history of mathematics.
    B. The photograph made the Eiffel Tower look like it was balanced on Oswald's palm.
    C. It is easy to get confused when calculating time differences between time zones a useful way to remember them is that the Atlantic Ocean starts with A, as in A.M., and the Pacific Ocean starts with P, as in P.M.
    D. No mistake.

11.

    A. Arnold was disappointed to discover the model airplane he purchased online was half the size he expected.
    B. Computer storage has come a long way since the days of punched paper tape.
    C. The surrealists were a group of artists who believed that art should reflect the subconscious mind, their images are often very dreamlike, showing businessmen falling like rain over a city and melting clocks.
    D. No mistake.

12.

    A. A "moor" is a plot of uncultivated land, similar to prairies in the U.S.
    B. "Orange is my favorite color, but not my favorite fruit." said Lisa.
    C. Some historians believe that the United States would have been too large for one government to control if the telegraph had not been invented in 1837.
    D. No mistake.

13.

A. The largest volcano in our solar system is found on Mars.
B. The deepest canyon, too.
C. The volcano, called the Olympus Mons, is 342 miles in width and 17 miles tall; the canyon, called the Valles Marinaris, is 2,500 miles long.
D. No mistake.

14.

A. Pocahontas spent the last year's of her young life in England under the name Rebecca.
B. Dorine beat me in tennis for three straight matches.
C. Much of the light given off by stars is blocked by cosmic dust before it reaches the Earth's atmosphere.
D. No mistake.

15.

A. The Pima Indians of Arizona have remarkably high rates of diabetes and obesity some scientists believe the gene that causes this present-day health crisis was actually of great value to the Pima's ancestors who had to be able to retain glucose during periods of famine.
B. Recent research has discovered that some types of incense can create effects in the human brain similar to antidepressants.
C. Though debate on the topic has been ongoing, some believe that many amphibian species may be on the brink of extinction.
D. No mistake.

16.

A. The driver's side fender of my car is caved in because the high-speed winds pulled the door open too quickly.
B. While there is some truth to the belief that Eskimos have many words for snow, it is often overlooked that there are quite a few words for snow in English too: snow, slush, flurry, snowflake, and even more if you count the slang of snowboarders.
C. Director Alfred Hitchcock make over 60 films in his career.
D. No mistake.

17.

A. A good pediatrician should try not to laugh at the fears of new parents.
B. Some of the most difficult words to spell include "bureaucracy," "sacrilegious," and "millennium."
C. Sales of digitally downloaded albums have risen from 5.5 million in 2004 to 65.8 million in 2008.
D. No mistake.

For Questions 18-21, select the answer that best combines the underlined sentences into one.

18. The Scottish Enlightenment began during the eighteenth century. The name of the movement reflects a period of growth throughout Scotland in the areas of philosophy, architecture, science, and the arts.

A. Because the Scottish Enlightenment began during the eighteenth century, the name of the movement reflects a period of growth throughout Scotland in the areas of philosophy, architecture, science, and the arts.
B. While the Scottish Enlightenment began during the eighteenth century, the name of the movement reflects a period of growth throughout Scotland in the areas of philosophy, architecture, science and the arts.
C. The Scottish Enlightenment began during the eighteenth century, but the name of the movement reflects a period of growth throughout Scotland in the areas of philosophy, architecture, science, and the arts.
D. The Scottish Enlightenment began during the eighteenth century and reflects a period of growth throughout Scotland in the areas of philosophy, architecture, science, and the arts.

19. Famous participants include Robert Burns. He was a poet who fused traditional folk songs with standard poetic forms.

A. Famous participants include Robert Burns, a poet who fused traditional folk songs with standard poetic forms.
B. Robert Burns was a Scottish poet who fused traditional folk songs with standard poetic forms.
C. Famous participants include Robert Burns, because he was a poet who fused traditional folk songs with standard poetic forms.
D. Robert Burns was a poet who fused traditional folk songs with standard poetic forms and was a famous participant in the Scottish Enlightenment.

20. Philosopher David Hume made his mark in the Scottish Enlightenment and in the study of philosophy for future generations. He was best known for his historical writings in his own day.

A. Philosopher David Hume made his mark in the Scottish Enlightenment and in the study of philosophy for future generations, and he was best known for his historical writings in his own day.
B. Philosopher David Hume made his mark in the Scottish Enlightenment and in the study of philosophy for future generations, but he was best known for his historical writings in his own day.
C. Since David Hume made his mark in the Scottish Enlightenment and in the study of philosophy for future generations, he was best known for his historical writings in his own day.
D. Philosopher David Hume made his mark in the Scottish Enlightenment and in the study of philosophy for future generations, as he was best known for his historical writings in his own day.

21. Joseph Black studied medicine at the University of Glasgow. He would go on to pursue experiments in chemistry that ultimately resulted in the isolation and identification of carbon dioxide.

A. Joseph Black studied medicine at the University of Glasgow, but he would go on to pursue experiments in chemistry that ultimately resulted in the isolation and identification of carbon dioxide.

B. Because Joseph Black studied medicine at the University of Glasgow, he would go on to pursue experiments in chemistry that ultimately resulted in the isolation and identification of carbon dioxide.

C. Although Joseph Black studied medicine at the University of Glasgow, he would go on to pursue experiments in chemistry that ultimately resulted in the isolation and identification of carbon dioxide.

D. After Joseph Black studied medicine at the University of Glasgow, he would go on to pursue experiments in chemistry that ultimately resulted in the isolation and identification of carbon dioxide.

For Questions 22-27, choose the best sentence to fill in the blank in the paragraph.

22. _____. The Crusades began when the Emperor Alexius I requested assistance against the Seljuk Turks who were encroaching upon the Byzantine Empire. But the eventual purpose of the Crusade focused on the Holy Land, and Jerusalem in particular, as the Crusaders attempted to force the Muslim princes out of the city and give it over to Christian rule. The popes sanctioned and encouraged the Crusades by providing wide-scale indulgences for Crusaders. The history of the Crusades was ultimately marked by both valor and violence in a struggle that placed religious struggles alongside political goals.

A. Between 1095 and 1291, the monarchs of Europe launched a series of Crusades to take over portions of the Near East.

B. The Crusades were military campaigns supported by the medieval Catholic Church for the purpose of driving Muslim rule out of the Near East.

C. While composed in part of Christian warriors seeking penance and favor with God, the Crusades were made up largely of mercenaries who sought only financial gain.

D. In spite of the fact that they were usually on opposing sides, Christian and Muslim warriors often had great respect for one another.

23. The First Crusade began when Pope Urban II asked for European Christians to help in defending the Eastern Christian, or Byzantine, empire against the invading Turks. The Crusaders started in a joint effort from both France and Italy in August of 1096. They fought successfully and saw the Byzantine city of Nicea come into Christian hands the following June. The Crusaders then took the city of Anatolia in October of 1097 and Antioch in June of 1098. Upon taking the city of Antioch, the Crusaders began massacring Muslim inhabitants and destroying Muslim religious centers. _____.

A. The Crusaders then suffered by starving on their way to Jerusalem.

B. The Crusaders had to join with the Muslims to defend the city of Jerusalem against Frankish mercenaries.

C. In the early stages of the siege at Antioch, the long-term Christian inhabitants were forced out of the city to prevent collusion with the Crusaders.

D. As a result, the Muslims responded with a counterattack that left the Crusader force largely decimated.

24. The Second Crusade did not begin until 1147. _____. In the mid-twelfth century, however, Muslims took the city of Edessa in modern-day Turkey. The French preacher Bernard of Clairveaux called upon Christian Crusaders to arm themselves once again. At the head of the Crusading army was the French King Louise VI and the German King Conrad III. Despite these illustrious brothers in arms, the Second Crusade was largely unsuccessful in the Holy Land. The primary result was the massacre of Jewish inhabitants in parts of Germany by passing Crusaders.

A. Until then, the Holy Land had seen a period of peace, with Christians living alongside Muslims.
B. Prior to this, there had been a brief Crusade under King Sigurd I of Norway to drive Muslims out of Spain.
C. The Crusaders began focusing on other cities besides Jerusalem for extending Christian rule.
D. At the time, there were approximately 120,000 European Christians living in Jerusalem, compared with 350,000 Eastern Christians, Muslims, and Jews.

25. _____. Pope Gregory VII encouraged Crusaders to take action against what he saw as an offense against Christendom, and the call was answered. King Philip II of France, King Richard I of England, and Holy Roman Emperor Frederick I led an army of eager warriors to Jerusalem. Along the way, the Crusaders successfully captured the island of Cyprus and the cities of Acre and Jaffa from the Muslims. They failed to take Jerusalem, however. The primary success of the Third Crusade was in establishing a treaty with Salāh ad-Dīn that enabled Christians to visit the city of Jerusalem for pilgrimages.

A. It was the success of the Egyptian Sultan Salāh ad-Dīn in conquering Jerusalem in 1187 that launched the Third Crusade.
B. The Third Crusade began in 1187 and was focused more on Jerusalem than the previous Crusades.
C. The Third Crusade, which started in 1187, might be the most famous for its noble participants.
D. Though ostensibly an enemy of the Crusaders, Salāh ad-Dīn was widely respected both as a powerful warrior and as an honorable ruler.

26. The Fourth Crusade resulted, however unintentionally at its start, in the final break between Eastern and Western Christianity. Pope Innocent III called for Crusaders again in 1202, but money was tight and expectations for success limited. To earn money, the Crusaders were commissioned to help restore the city of Zara, or Zadar, in modern-day Croatia. The warriors were unhappy with this situation and pushed on to the Byzantine city of Constantinople. While in Constantinople, these soldiers who had once been Crusaders pillaged and largely destroyed the city in 1204. _____.

A. The Latin Empire that followed the Byzantine Empire portioned off the Byzantine territories to Crusaders.
B. The Fourth Crusade might have ended much differently had the problem of funding been solved early on.
C. The schism that had been separating the Eastern Church from the Western Church for centuries was finally confirmed after the sacking of Constantinople.
D. It was the offense of working for the Venetian Doge Enrico Dandolo that drove the Crusaders to such brutality against the Eastern Empire.

27. The Fifth Crusade began as a result of the decisions from the Fourth Council of the Lateran, under Pope Innocent III, in 1215. _____. The first phase would assist the (Christian) kings of Jerusalem and Antioch in taking Jerusalem from the Muslims and returning it to Christian authority. The second phase would take the Egyptian city of Damietta, which is an important port in the Nile Delta. The Crusaders were successful up to this point in the phases of the Fifth Crusade but exceeded in their ambitions when they tried to take Cairo. The Egyptian Sultan al-Kamil stopped their progress but did agree to a treaty for eight years of peace with Europe.

   A. Pope Innocent had been disappointed in the results of the Fourth Crusade and wanted to see better successes in a fresh attempt.
   B. The Lateran Council had determined a need to reclaim the Holy Land for Christendom and created two separate phases for accomplishing this task.
   C. The primary crusading forces for the Fifth Crusade would come out of Austria and Hungary.
   D. St. Francis of Assisi would play a vital role in the Fifth Crusade, in helping establish peace in the Holy Land.

For Questions 28 and 29, choose the best sentence to follow and develop the topic sentence that is given.

28. The practice of alchemy is believed to date back to ancient Egypt.

   A. It was the Hellenistic Egyptians who noted the roots in early Egyptian practice.
   B. Alchemy grew in popularity during the Middle Ages, with such scholars as Paracelsus and Roger Bacon.
   C. The fourth-century scientist Zosimos of Panalopolis claimed that ancient Egyptian priests practiced alchemy in their work.
   D. Some historians have found roots of alchemy in China as well.

29. Medieval alchemy developed as a combination of scientific traditions, as well as religious and mystical beliefs.

   A. Many practices among alchemists were believed to be immoral, and both popes and kings banned alchemist activities.
   B. Alchemists were believed to subvert the natural order and were frequently portrayed as defying God.
   C. In the modern world, alchemy is considered to be a false science that prevented real scientific advances during the Middle Ages.
   D. Alchemists worked to combine teachings from faith and science, drawing from the works of both St. Anselm and Plato.

For questions 30 and 31, select the sentence that does not belong in the paragraph.

30. Which sentence does not belong in the following paragraph?

1] Though Thomas Jefferson's taste for expensive home furnishings and wine contributed to the substantial debts he faced toward the end of his life, many other factors also contributed. 2] For instance, when Jefferson's father-in-law died, all of his debts were transferred to Jefferson. 3] Additionally, though his holdings in land and slaves were considerable, they were never especially profitable. 4] Jefferson is believed to have fathered children with one of his slaves. 5] Finally, less than a decade before his death, Jefferson unwisely agreed to endorse a $20,000 loan for a friend, and when the friend unexpectedly died a year later, Jefferson inherited yet another large debt. 6] Jefferson's personal experience with debt may have been part of his motivation in criticizing policies that would increase the national debt.

A. Sentence 2
B. Sentence 3
C. Sentence 4
D. Sentence 5

31. Which sentence does not belong in the following paragraph?

1] Renowned scientist Richard Feynman once said that the atomic theory is the most profound discoveries scientists have made. 2] Feynman was also an accomplished percussionist who could play nine beats with one hand while playing ten with the other! 3] "All things are made of atoms," explained Feynman, "little particles that…move around in perpetual motion, attracting each other when they are a little distance apart, but repelling upon being squeezed into one another." 4] He then made the claim that this idea is one of the most illuminating ideas in the history of science: "In that one sentence, you will see, there is an enormous amount of information about the world, if just a little imagination and thinking are applied. "

A. Sentence 1
B. Sentence 2
C. Sentence 3
D. Sentence 4

For Questions 32-54, read the sentence and select the correctly written answer to replace each underlined sentence or phrase.

32. Several theories <u>about what caused dinosaurs to have extinction exist</u>, but scientists are still unable to reach a concrete conclusion.

A. about what caused dinosaurs to have extinction exist
B. about what caused dinosaurs to become extinct exist
C. about the causes of the dinosaur extinction exists
D. regarding the cause of extinction of dinosaurs exist

33. <u>Although most persons</u> prefer traditional pets like cats and dogs, others gravitate towards exotic animals like snakes and lizards.

    A. Although most persons
    B. Because most people
    C. While most people
    D. Maybe some persons

34. It is important that software companies offer tech support <u>to customers who are encountering problems</u>.

    A. to customers who are encountering problems
    B. because not all customers encounter problems
    C. with customers who encounter problems
    D. to customer who is encountering difficulties

35. The fact <u>that children eat high fat diets and watch excessive amount of television are a cause of concern</u> for many parents.

    A. that children eat high fat diets and watch excessive amount of television are a cause of concern
    B. the children eat high fat diets and watches excessive amount of television are a cause of concern
    C. is children eat high fat diets and watch excessive amount of television is a cause for concern
    D. that children eat high fat diets and watch excessive amounts of television is a cause for concern

36. <u>Contrarily to popular beliefs</u>, bats do not actually entangle themselves in the hair of humans on purpose.

    A. Contrarily to popular beliefs
    B. Contrary to popular belief
    C. Contrary to popularity belief
    D. Contrary to popular believing

37. <u>Considering how long ago the Ancient Egyptians lived, it's amazing</u> we know anything about them at all.

    A. Considering how long ago the Ancient Egyptians lived, it's amazing
    B. Consider how long the Ancient Egyptians lived, it's amazing
    C. Considering for how long the Ancient Egyptians lived, its amazing
    D. Considering, how long ago the Ancient Egyptians lived, its amazing

38. <u>Because technology has constantly changed</u>, those employed in the IT industry must learn new skills continuously.

    A. Because technology has constantly changed
    B. Because technology is constantly changing
    C. Even though technology is changing
    D. Despite the fact that technology has changed

39. <u>To mix, shade, and highlighting</u> are essential skills that every beginning artist must master.

    A. To mix, shade, and highlighting
    B. Mix, shade, and highlighting
    C. To mixing, shading, and highlighting
    D. Mixing, shading, and highlighting

40. The growing problem of resistance to antibiotics can be attributed, in part, <u>to the fact that they are prescribed unnecessarily</u>.

    A. to the fact that they are prescribed unnecessarily
    B. in the facts that they are prescribed unnecessarily
    C. to the fact that they are prescribing unnecessarily
    D. with the facts that they are being prescribed unnecessarily.

41. <u>A key challenges facing university graduates</u> searching for employment is that most have limited work experience.

    A. A key challenges facing university graduates
    B. Key challenge faced by university graduates
    C. A key challenge facing university graduates
    D. Key challenges facing university's graduates

42. Children who aren't nurtured during infancy are more likely to develop attachment disorders, <u>which can cause persisting and severely problems</u> later in life.

    A. which can cause persisting and severely problems
    B. that can cause persisting and severe problem
    C. they can cause persistent and severe problem
    D. which can cause persistent and severe problems

43. While speed is a measure of how fast an object is moving, velocity measures how fast an object is moving <u>and also indicates in what direction</u> it is traveling.

    A. and also indicates in what direction
    B. and only indicates in which direction
    C. and also indicate in which directions
    D. and only indicated in what direction

44. Many companies are now using social networking sites like Facebook and MySpace <u>to market there service and product.</u>

    A. to market there service and product
    B. to market their services and products
    C. and market their service and products
    D. which market their services and products

45. An autoclave is a tool used mainly in hospitals <u>to sterilizing surgical tools and hypodermic needles</u>.

    A. to sterilizing surgical tools and hypodermic needles
    B. for sterilize surgical tools and hypodermic needles
    C. to sterilize surgical tools and hypodermic needles
    D. for sterilizing the surgical tool and hypodermic needle

46. The bizarre creatures known by electric eels are capable of emitting an incredible 600 volts of electricity.

    A. The bizarre creatures known by electric eels
    B. A bizarre creature known as electric eels
    C. The bizarre creatures known to electric eels
    D. The bizarre creatures known as electric eels

47. A key factor taken into account during city planning is where major services and amenities will be located.

    A. A key factor taken into account during city planning is
    B. Key factors taken into account during city planning is
    C. A key factor taking into account during city planning is
    D. Key factors, taken into accounting during city planning are

48. Jupiter with its numerous moons, and Great Red Spot, has been studied extensively by astronomers.

    A. Jupiter with its numerous moons, and Great Red Spot,
    B. Jupiter with, its numerous moons and Great Red Spot,
    C. Jupiter, with its numerous moons and Great Red Spot,
    D. Jupiter with, its numerous moons, and Great Red Spot,

49. Many gardeners are now making their own backyard compost, which is not only cheap, but also helps to cut down on landfill waste.

    A. which is not only cheap, but also helps to cut down on landfill waste
    B. which is not only cheaper, but also cuts down on landfill's waste
    C. which is, not only cheap, but also, helps to cut down on landfill waste
    D. which is not only done cheaply, but is also cutting down on landfills wastes

50. The growth of the security industry can be large attributable to the fact that people are less trusting of others than they once were.

    A. The growth of the security industry can be large attributable
    B. The growing of the securities industry can be largely attributable
    C. The growth on the security industry can be large attributed
    D. The growth of the security industry can be largely attributed

51. Claude Monet was a famous painter who's well-known painting includes *San Giorgio Maggiore at Dusk* and *The Water Lily Pond.*.

    A. who's well-known painting includes
    B. whose well-known painting including
    C. whose well-known paintings include
    D. who well-known paintings include

52. If he stops to consider the ramifications of this decision, it is probable that he will rethink his original decision a while longer.

    A. it is probable that he will rethink his original decision.
    B. he will rethink his original decision over again.
    C. he probably will rethink his original decision.
    D. he will most likely rethink his original decision for a bit.

53. "When you get <u>older," she said "you will no doubt</u> understand what I mean."

    A. older," she said "you will no doubt
    B. older" she said "you will no doubt
    C. older," she said, "you will no doubt
    D. older," she said "you will not

54. Dr. Anderson strolled past the nurses, examining a bottle of pills.

    A. Dr. Anderson strolled past the nurses, examining a bottle of pills.
    B. Dr. Anderson strolled past the nurses examining a bottle of pills.
    C. Dr. Anderson strolled past, the nurses examining a bottle of pills.
    D. Examining a bottle of pills, Dr. Anderson strolled past the nurses.

Reading Skills Practice Questions

Questions 1 to 4 pertain to the following passage:

It is most likely that you have never had diphtheria. You probably don't even know anyone who has suffered from this disease. In fact, you may not even know what diphtheria is. Similarly, diseases like whooping cough, measles, mumps, and rubella may all be unfamiliar to you. In the nineteenth and early twentieth centuries, these illnesses struck hundreds of thousands of people in the United States each year, mostly children, and tens of thousands of people died. The names of these diseases were frightening household words. Today, they are all but forgotten. That change happened largely because of vaccines.

You probably have been vaccinated against diphtheria. You may even have been exposed to the bacterium that causes it, but the vaccine prepared your body to fight off the disease so quickly that you were unaware of the infection. Vaccines take advantage of your body's natural ability to learn how to combat many disease-causing germs, or microbes. What's more, your body remembers how to protect itself from the microbes it has encountered before. Collectively, the parts of your body that remember and repel microbes are called the immune system. Without the proper functioning of the immune system, the simplest illness—even the common cold—could quickly turn deadly.

On average, your immune system needs more than a week to learn how to fight off an unfamiliar microbe. Sometimes, that isn't enough time. Strong microbes can spread through your body faster than the immune system can fend them off. Your body often gains the upper hand after a few weeks, but in the meantime you are sick. Certain microbes are so virulent that they can overwhelm or escape your natural defenses. In those situations, vaccines can make all the difference.

Traditional vaccines contain either parts of microbes or whole microbes that have been altered so that they don't cause disease. When your immune system confronts these harmless versions of the germs, it quickly clears them from your body. In other words, vaccines trick your immune system in order to teach your body important lessons about how to defeat its opponents.

1. What is the main idea of the passage?

    A. The nineteenth and early twentieth centuries were a dark period for medicine.
    B. You have probably never had diphtheria.
    C. Traditional vaccines contain altered microbes.
    D. Vaccines help the immune system function properly.

2. Which statement is *not* a detail from the passage?

    A. Vaccines contain microbe parts or altered microbes.
    B. The immune system typically needs a week to learn how to fight a new disease.
    C. The symptoms of disease do not emerge until the body has learned how to fight the microbe.
    D. A hundred years ago, children were at the greatest risk of dying from now-treatable diseases.

3. What is the meaning of the word *virulent* as it is used in the third paragraph?

    A. tiny
    B. malicious
    C. contagious
    D. annoying

4. What is the author's primary purpose in writing the essay?

    A. to entertain
    B. to persuade
    C. to inform
    D. to analyze

Answer questions 5 through 9 based on the jobs-wanted ads below.

City of Elm Babysitting/ Nanny Jobs Wanted	
College sophomore, aged 20, seeks regular part-time nanny work. Weekends (Sat and Sun) only. Up to three kids, any age range. Have four years of babysitting experience. References available. Contact Lisa, 634-1966.	Very responsible and reliable high-school junior available for occasional babysitting. I love kids and they love me! Personal references available. Contact Jose at 422-6868.
Experienced nanny seeks full-time (M-F, 9-5) nanny position. Over 10 years' experience as nanny. Many, including local, references available. Will also consider light housework, cooking. Contact James. 212-1736.	Devoted, experienced, reliable nanny seeks part-time (Tuesday and Thursday) nanny work. Also available for occasional evening and weekend childcare. Contact Regina at 530-1227.

5. If the Malbec family is looking for occasional weekend childcare, which of the people seeking work should they contact?

    A. Lisa and James
    B. Jose and James
    C. James and Regina
    D. Lisa and Regina

6. If the Bright family needs a babysitter for a single Friday night, which of the people seeking work should they contact?

    A. Lisa and Jose
    B. Regina and James
    C. Regina and Jose
    D. Lisa and James

7. If the Sulinus need a two-day-a-week babysitter for their four kids, which of the people seeking work is their best choice to contact?

    A. Lisa
    B. Jose
    C. James
    D. Regina

8. According to the ads, which of the people seeking work might also cook dinners for the Canterruni family if that person was hired for childcare?

    A. Lisa
    B. Jose
    C. James
    D. Regina

9. Which of the people seeking work can one infer from the ads is the youngest?

    A. Lisa
    B. Jose
    C. James
    D. Regina

Answer questions 10-12 based on the chart below.

Betty's Boutique Sales Report
(sales amounts in thousands of dollars)

Department	1 Qtr 2008	2 Qtr 2008	3 Qtr 2008	4 Qtr 2008	1 Qtr 2009
Women's wear	157	153	153	149	157
Men's wear	96	90	87	86	88
Children	63	55	56	54	57
Accessories	85	81	76	73	73
Shoes	70	68	68	67	68
Hair and Body	66	59	60	57	61

10. Which department's sales decreased by the biggest percentage from first quarter 2008 to first quarter 2009?

    A. Women's wear
    B. Accessories
    C. Shoes
    D. Hair and Body

11. During which quarter were overall store sales the lowest?

    A. 1st quarter 2008
    B. 2nd quarter 2008
    C. 3rd quarter 2008
    D. 4th quarter 2008

12. Which department's sales are back, in first quarter 2009, to what they were in first quarter 2008?

    A. Women's wear
    B. Men's wear
    C. Accessories
    D. All of the above

Use the advertisement below to answer questions 13 – 15.

Job Description:

Assistant City Attorney– City of Elm

The City of Elm is now hiring for the position of assistant City Attorney, litigation. Candidates must be members in Good Standing of the California Bar Association. Ideal candidates will have:

- at least 3 years litigation experience
- the ability to work both self-directed and as part of a team
- the ability to manage a large caseload

Competitive salary and excellent benefits offered. Position available immediately.

Send completed application to:

HR Department

Attention Veronica Smith

1 City Center Plaza

Elm, California 95763

13. According to the advertisement, which of the following is true?
    A. Candidates must have three or more years litigation experience
    B. Candidates will have small caseloads
    C. Candidates must be members of the California State Bar Association
    D. The position is not currently available

14. A "competitive salary" is one that is
    A. Much less than salaries offered for comparable jobs
    B. Much greater than salaries offered for comparable jobs
    C. Similar to the average salary offered for comparable jobs
    D. Impossible to compare to the salaries offered for comparable jobs

15. It can be inferred from the advertisement that
    A. A person staffing this position may work independently and/or as part of a team.
    B. Veronica Davis will make the hiring decisions.
    C. Caseloads will start out small for new hires.
    D. A candidate could work part-time if he or she chose to.

Use the radio schedule below to answer questions 16 through 20.

Sunday May 17	
Overnight	
12 a.m.	News from the BBC World headlines from BBC London.
1 a.m.	California Update Upcoming election discussed.
2 a.m.	Money Matters How to protect your retirement if you lose your job.
3 a.m.	Commonwealth Club The Green Economy. Host Stephen Sanders speaks with Nancy Sparks, leading proponent of the idea that green jobs can save the world economy.
4 a.m.	News from the BBC World headlines from BBC London.
5 a.m.	All About Art Host Guy Phillips speaks to three local graffiti artists.
Morning	
7 a.m.	California Update Upcoming election discussed.
9 a.m.	Smart Talk Call-in show about President Obama's first 100 days in office.
10 a.m.	Car Talk Tom & Ray Magliozzi host a call-in show about your car problems.
11 a.m.	Prairie Home Companion Garrison Keillor.

16. What show features talk about an upcoming election?

    A. News from the BBC
    B. California Update
    C. Commonwealth Club
    D. Smart Talk

17. Which two shows state that they are call-in shows?

    A. Smart Talk and Car Talk
    B. Smart Talk and California Update
    C. Car Talk and Prairie Home Companion
    D. All About Art and California Update

18. From the information given, on which show would you expect to hear the most discussion about national U.S. politics?

    A. News from the BBC
    B. California Update
    C. Smart Talk
    D. Commonwealth Club

19. On which show would you expect to hear the environment discussed the most?

    A. Prairie Home Companion
    B. Commonwealth Club
    C. California Update
    D. News from the BBC

20. On which show would you be most likely to hear the following "should drawing on someone else's property without their consent be treated as a crime?"

    A. California Report
    B. Car Talk
    C. Commonwealth Club
    D. All About Art

Use the information on the train timetable below to answer questions 21 through 26.

Fremont – Richmond Line					
Fremont	**Union City**	**S. Hayward**	**Hayward**	**Bay Fair**	**San Leandro**
7:45	7:50	7:55	7:59	8:03	8:07
8:00	8:05	8:10	8:14	8:18	8:22
8:15	8:20	8:25	8:29	8:33	8:37
8:30	8:35	8:40	8:44	8:48	8:52
8:45	8:50	8:55	8:59	9:03	9:07

21. If you need to be in Bay Fair by 8:45, what is the latest train you could take leaving Union City?

    A. 7:50
    B. 8:00
    C. 8:20
    D. 8:35

22. How many stops will you make *before* arriving in San Leandro if you get on the line in Union City?

    A. 1
    B. 2
    C. 3
    D. 4

23. Which is the longest trip?

    A. Union City to South Hayward
    B. South Hayward to Hayward
    C. Hayward to Bay Fair
    D. Bay Fair to San Leandro

24. Which is the shortest trip?

    A. Fremont to Hayward
    B. Union City to Bay Fair
    C. South Hayward to San Leandro
    D. Hayward to Bay Fair

- 18 -

25. If you need to be in Hayward at 8:50, what is the latest train you could take leaving Fremont?

    A. 7:45

    B. 8:00

    C. 8:15

    D. 8:30

26. If someone tells you their regular ride takes exactly four minutes, which route are they *not* taking?

    A. Fremont to Union City

    B. South Hayward to Hayward

    C. Hayward to Bay Fair

    D. Bay Fair to San Leandro

Questions 27 through 29 refer to the following passage:

    Street newspapers are newspapers that are sold primarily by homeless people and primarily focus on homelessness issues. Some of the newspapers are written by homeless people, thus the papers seek to give such populations both an income and a voice in policy and popular discussions about homelessness and poverty in general. Concern over mainstream media portrayal of homelessness and the homeless (as drug addicts and/or criminals and/or simply lazy) was partly the reason for the emergence of these papers in the United States. Most papers operate by selling the papers to the homeless vendors for some percentage of the list price; the vendor then gets to keep the proceeds from all sales.

27. What is a reason cited by the passage for the emergence of the street newspapers?

    A. Homeless people were writing articles that they sought to have published

    B. Homeless people get to keep proceeds from all sales

    C. Homeless people get a voice in policy discussions about homelessness

    D. There was concern over mainstream media portrayal of homelessness

28. According to the passage, who sells the street newspapers?

    A. Homeless men and women

    B. Primarily homeless men and women

    C. People who are not homeless

    D. Passage does not state

29. What money do the vendors net from their work selling the papers?

    A. A percentage of the list price

    B. The entire list price

    C. The list price for which they sell the paper minus the percentage they pay of the list price

    D. Nothing, they do it for free

Questions 30 – 33 refer to the following passage:

    Among the Atkins, South Beach and other diets people embark upon for health and weight loss is the so-called Paleolithic Diet in which adherents eat what they believe to be a diet similar to that consumed by humans during the Paleolithic era. The diet consists of food that can be hunted or gathered: primarily of meat, fish, vegetables, fruits, roots, and nuts. It does not allow for grains, legumes, dairy, salt, refined sugars or processed oils. The idea behind the diet is that humans are genetically adapted to the diet of our Paleolithic forebears. Some studies support the idea of positive health outcomes from such a diet.

30. Which of the following does the passage not give as the name of a diet?

   A. South Beach
   B. Hunter Gatherer
   C. Paleolithic
   D. Atkins

31. Which of the following is not permitted on the Paleolithic Diet?

   A. meat
   B. dairy
   C. vegetables
   D. nuts

32. What does the passage say is the idea behind the diet?

   A. That humans are genetically adapted to the diet of our Paleolithic forebears
   B. That it increases health
   C. That it supports weight loss
   D. That it consists of food that can be hunted or gathered

33. Which of the following does the passage suggest is true?

   A. No studies support the claim that the Paleolithic Diet promotes health
   B. Some studies support the claim that the Paleolithic Diet promotes health
   C. All studies support the claim that the Paleolithic Diet promotes health
   D. No studies have been done on whether the Paleolithic Diet promotes health

Questions 34-37 refer to the passage below:

> Information for parents: We want to make your child's stay at Camp Yahali a truly happy, comfortable, and fulfilling one. To that end, we have developed what we believe to be the perfect balance of free time and structured activities. The activities cover a wide range of interests and we ask that you take a moment to sit down with your child to determine which activities your child would like to participate in and let us know by signing up prior to camp starting. That way we can make sure that we have enough supplies, equipment, and staff available for each of the activities. If there's room, we can do some limited changes at camp, but your child should expect to participate in the activities he or she signs up for. For this reason, we encourage you to make careful decisions about what to choose; some parents find it helpful to have their kids consult with their friends to make sure the activities are one that kids they know are also participating in.

34. What is the balance that the Camp Yahali staff describe?

   A. A balance between activities that suit different interests
   B. A balance between deciding on activities in advance and when at camp
   C. A balance between staffing for the different activities
   D. A balance between free time and structured activities

35. Why does the staff at Camp Yahali want to know which activities the kids want to participate in?

    A. So they can ensure there are enough supplies, equipment and staff
    B. So they can tell the kids' friends
    C. To encourage careful decision making
    D. To make the child's stay at Camp Yahali a happy, comfortable and fulfilling one

36. What can be inferred about why the staff at Camp Yahali suggests kids find out what activities their friends are participating in?

    A. It's important to ensure there are enough supplies, equipment and staff
    B. Kids will want to do activities with their friends
    C. Parents are curious
    D. Camp Yahali staff want kids to do activities only with their friends

37. Are changes in activity sign-up permitted once the child gets to camp?

    A. Yes, any changes a child wants
    B. No, no changes are permitted
    C. Yes, changes are permitted if the parent asks for them
    D. Yes, limited changes are permitted if there's room available

Questions 38-44 refer to the passage below:

VISUAL PERCEPTION

It is tempting to think that your eyes are simply mirrors that reflect whatever is in front of them. Researchers, however, have shown that your brain is constantly working to create the impression of a continuous, uninterrupted world.

For instance, in the last ten minutes, you have blinked your eyes around 200 times. You have probably not been aware of any of these interruptions in your visual world. Something you probably have not seen in a long time without the aid of a mirror is your nose. It is always right there, down in the bottom corner of your vision, but your brain filters it out so that you are not aware of your nose unless you purposefully look at it.

Nor are you aware of the artery that runs right down the middle of your retina. It creates a large blind spot in your visual field, but you never notice the hole it leaves. To see this blind spot, try the following: Cover your left eye with your hand. With your right eye, look at the O on the left. As you move your head closer to the O, the X will disappear as it enters the blind spot caused by your optical nerve.

O   X

Your brain works hard to make the world look continuous!

38. The word <u>filters</u>, as used in this passage, most nearly means:

    A. Alternates
    B. Reverses
    C. Ignores
    D. Depends

39. The word <u>retina</u>, as used in this passage, most nearly means:

    A. Optical illusion
    B. Part of the eye
    C. Pattern
    D. Blindness

40. Which of the following statements can be inferred from this passage?

    A. Not all animals' brains filter out information.
    B. Visual perception is not a passive process.
    C. Blind spots cause accidents.
    D. The eyes never reflect reality.

41. What is the author's purpose for including the two letters in the middle of the passage?

    A. To demonstrate the blind spot in the visual field.
    B. To organize the passage.
    C. To transition between the last two paragraphs of the passage.
    D. To prove that the blind spot is not real.

42. What is the main purpose of this passage?

    A. To persuade the reader to pay close attention to blind spots.
    B. To explain the way visual perception works.
    C. To persuade the reader to consult an optometrist if the O and X disappear.
    D. To prove that vision is a passive process.

43. Based on the passage, which of the following statements is true?

    A. The brain cannot accurately reflect reality.
    B. Glasses correct the blind spot caused by the optical nerve.
    C. Vision is the least important sense.
    D. The brain fills in gaps in the visual field.

44. The author mentions the nose to illustrate what point?

    A. The brain filters out some visual information.
    B. Not all senses work the same way.
    C. Perception is a passive process.
    D. The sense of smell filters out information.

Mathematics Computation Practice Questions

1. 3,306 + 2,794
   A. 5,090
   B. 5,100
   C. 6,090
   D. 6,100

2. 8,537 - 6,316
   A. 1,221
   B. 2,221
   C. 2,243
   D. 2,841

3. 643 × 72
   A. 44,096
   B. 44,186
   C. 46,296
   D. 45,576

4. 806 × 34
   A. 26,404
   B. 26,424
   C. 27,404
   D. 27,424

5. $5\overline{)854}$
   A. 170
   B. 170 R4
   C. 178
   D. 178 R4

6. $63\overline{)18144}$
   A. 256
   B. 258
   C. 286
   D. 288

7. $\frac{72}{1000}$ as a decimal
   A. 7.2
   B. 0.072
   C. 0.72
   D. 7.02

8. 0.19×0.23
   A. 0.3470
   B. 0.4370
   C. 0.0347
   D. 0.0437

9. $\frac{.3}{.08}$ *is equal to*:
   A. 0.0375
   B. 0.375
   C. 3.75
   D. 37.5

10. 0.43-0.17
    A. 0.26
    B. 2.6
    C. 0.36
    D. 3.6

11. $2\frac{1}{2} + 3 + \frac{1}{7}$
    A. $5\frac{9}{14}$
    B. $6\frac{1}{2}$
    C. $5\frac{5}{14}$
    D. $6\frac{5}{7}$

12. $3\frac{1}{9} - 1\frac{1}{4} =$
    A. $1\frac{5}{6}$
    B. $1\frac{31}{36}$
    C. $2\frac{5}{36}$
    D. $2\frac{31}{36}$

13. $3\frac{1}{8} \times 6\frac{1}{3} \times 2\frac{2}{5}$
    A. $47\frac{1}{2}$
    B. $36\frac{7}{8}$
    C. $40\frac{3}{8}$
    D. $42\frac{4}{5}$

14. $\frac{1}{8} \div \frac{4}{5}$

   A. $\frac{5}{32}$

   B. $\frac{1}{10}$

   C. $\frac{2}{5}$

   D. $\frac{3}{8}$

15. Which of the following is correct?

   A. $\frac{2}{3} = \frac{18}{24}$

   B. $\frac{4}{5} = \frac{16}{20}$

   C. $\frac{1}{9} = \frac{4}{18}$

   D. $\frac{3}{8} = \frac{9}{16}$

16. Find N for the following:

$$\frac{n}{5} = \frac{12}{20}$$

   A. 2
   B. 3
   C. 4
   D. 5

17. Reduce $\frac{17}{102}$ to lowest terms.

   A. $\frac{1}{4}$

   B. $\frac{5}{6}$

   C. $\frac{1}{6}$

   D. $\frac{3}{4}$

18. Express 99/14 as a mixed fraction.

   A. $7\frac{1}{14}$

   B. $7\frac{3}{14}$

   C. $7\frac{11}{14}$

   D. $7\frac{5}{14}$

19. 30% of 900

   A. 270
   B. 300
   C. 27
   D. 30

20. 2 = (?)% of 40

    A. 5

    B. 8

    C. 20

    D. 25

21. Three fifths of sixty equals:

    A. 30

    B. 32

    C. 36

    D. 40

22. .5% of 40=

    A. 0.2

    B. 0.8

    C. 2.0

    D. 8.0

23. Ratio of 2 to 10 = (?)%

    A. 2

    B. 3

    C. 5

    D. 20

24. $\frac{3}{10} = (?)\% \; x \frac{3}{4}$

    A. 25

    B. 30

    C. 35

    D. 40

25. $\frac{36}{9}$ as a percentage

    A. 4%

    B. 400%

    C. 40%

    D. 0.4%

26. 4:25 as a percentage

    A. 6.25%

    B. 0.625%

    C. 1.6%

    D. 16%

27. 15% as a reduced common fraction

    A. $\frac{3}{20}$

    B. $\frac{15}{100}$

    C. $\frac{5}{20}$

    D. $\frac{20}{3}$

28. 15% as a decimal

    A. 0.15
    B. 15.0
    C. 1.5
    D. 0.0015

29. 60 is 30% of (?)

    A. 90
    B. 180
    C. 200
    D. 210

30. $1\frac{1}{4}\% \ of \ (?) = 15$

    A. 80
    B. 120
    C. 140
    D. 150

31. 8 is 25% of x

    A. 16
    B. 24
    C. 32
    D. 40

32. 40% of x=18

    A. 36
    B. 360
    C. 45
    D. 450

33. $-7a + 4a + 5a$

    A. a
    B. $2a$
    C. $6a$
    D. $16a$

34. $(x^2 + 2x + 2) - (x^2 + 3x + 6)$

    A. 8+x
    B. 5x+8
    C. x-4
    D. 8-x

35. $3y + 6 = 30$

    A. $y = 3$
    B. y = 8
    C. $y = 4$
    D. $y = 12$

36. $5(x + 2) = 3(x + 4)$

    A. $x = 1$
    B. $x = 2$
    C. $x = 3$
    D. $x = 5$

37. $3ax^2 - 6ax^2$

    A. $3ax^2$
    B. $-3ax^2$
    C. $9ax^2$
    D. $-9ax^2$

38. $7(x + 3) - 3 + 3(x + 1)$

    A. $4x + 3$
    B. $4x + 21$
    C. $10x + 21$
    D. $10x + 27$

39. $3x - 6 = 15$

    A. $x = 5$
    B. $x = 6$
    C. $x = 7$
    D. $x = 8$

40. $2(r + 3) + 2 = (r + 6)3$

    A. $r = 4$
    B. $r = -4$
    C. $r = 10$
    D. $r = -10$

Applied Mathematics Practice Questions

1. Which of the following numbers is greatest?

    A. 1/3
    B. 0.25
    C. 0.099
    D. 2/7

2. Which number is 300% of the difference between 23 and 27?

    A. 4
    B. 75
    C. 12
    D. 25

3. Which number should come next in the series: 4, 13, 22, 31, ...?

    A. 40
    B. 39
    C. 34
    D. 42

4. What number is one half the average of 3, 4, and 5?

    A. 1.5
    B. 2
    C. 4
    D. 2.5

5. Examine the figure below, which shows two lines passing through the center O of a circle, and select the best answer.

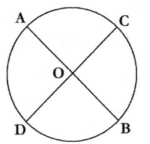

    A. AO is greater than OC but less than CD
    B. AB is greater than CD and greater than DO
    C. AB is greater than OC but less than CD
    D. AO is the same length as OC but less than CD

6. A music download takes 15 minutes for the first 20%. If it continues at the same rate, what will be the total amount of time required to download the entire piece of music?

    A. 1 hour 15 minutes
    B. 1 hour
    C. 50 minutes
    D. 45 minutes

7. An airplane travels at 300 mph relative to the air. It moves against a headwind of 15 mph. what is its speed relative to the ground?

    A. 300 mph
    B. 315 mph
    C. 270 mph
    D. 285 mph

8. There are an equal number of boys and girls in Mrs. McCarthy's class. The average height of the boys is 110 cm. The average height of the entire class is 105 cm. What is the average height, in centimeters, of the girls in Mrs. McCarthy's class?

    A. 90 cm
    B. 95 cm
    C. 100 cm
    D. 105 cm

9. Examine (a), (b), and (c) and select the best answer.

(a) $\dfrac{3}{5}$ (b) $\dfrac{40}{50}$ c) $\dfrac{8}{50}$

    A. (a) > (b) > (c)
    B. (a) = (b) =(c)
    C. (a) < (b) and (b)> (c)
    D. (a) < (b) and (b)<(c)

10. Which of the following is equal to the difference between 4^3 and 3^4?

    A. 0
    B. 1
    C. 27
    D. 17

11. Which of the following choices is the missing number from this series: 1, 2, 4, __, 16?

    A. 6
    B. 8
    C. 10
    D. 12

12. Consider the figures below and select the best answer. Assume all circles are equal in size and that the chords in the circles are diameters.

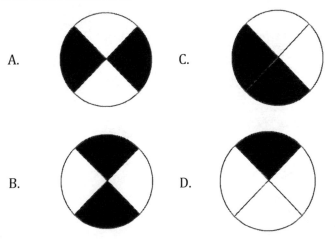

A. The shaded areas in (a) and (b) are equal and less than the shaded area in (c)
B. The shaded area in (a) is greater than the shaded area in (d) and less than the shaded area in (c)
C. The shaded areas in (a), (b), and (c) are all equal.
D. The shaded areas in all four diagrams are equal.

13. Which of the following numbers is the smallest?

A. 2^8
B. 3^3
C. 16^1
D. 24

14. Which number comes next in the series: 12, 7, 8, 13, 4, 19, 0, ... ?

A. 25
B. 0
C. 19
D. -2

15. Examine (a), (b), and (c) and find the best answer.
(a) 20% of 80 (b) 50% of 70   (c) 40% of 90

A. (b)>(c)
B. (b)>(a)
C. (a)<(b) and (b)=(c)
D. (a)=(b)=(c)

16. Which number is three times as much as 3^2?

A. 9
B. 18
C. 27
D. 30

- 31 -

17. Which number is 3 more than $\dfrac{4}{5}$ of 30?

    A. 27
    B. 18
    C. 33
    D. 29

18. Which of the following sums is the greatest?
    A. 3 + 4 + 16
    B. 6 + 4 + 5 + 7
    C. 4 + 5 + 9
    D. 10 + 4 + 8

19. Examine (a), (b), and (c) and find the best answer.

$$\text{(a) } \dfrac{1}{3} \text{ of } 24 \quad \text{(b) } \dfrac{1}{5} \text{ of } 30 \quad \text{(c) } \dfrac{3}{4} \text{ of } 20$$

    A. (b)<(c)
    B. (a)<(b)<(c)
    C. (a)=(b) and (b)<(c)
    D. (a)=(b) and (b)>(c)

20. Examine (a), (b), and (c) and find the best answer. Consider only the magnitude of each measurement.

    (a) The perimeter of a rectangle with length of 6 cm and width of 4 cm
    (b) The perimeter of a square with sides 4 cm long
    (c) The area of a square with sides 4 cm long

    A. (b)>(c)
    B. (a)=(b)=(c)
    C. (b)=(c)
    D. (b)<(c)

21. What is the difference between 45 and the average of 20, 35, 45, and 20?
    A. 0
    B. 15
    C. 17
    D. 20

22. The mean of 3 numbers is 11. Two of the numbers are 8 and 13. What is the third number?
    A. 11
    B. 13
    C. 12
    D. 10

23. Examine (a), (b), and (c) and find the best answer.

(a) $\dfrac{2}{3}$ (b) $\dfrac{20}{30}$ (c) $\dfrac{30}{45}$

A. (b)>(c)
B. (a)=(b)=(c)
C. (b)=(c)
D. (b)<(c)

24. Examine (a), (b), and (c) and find the best answer.

(a) (3 x 4) + 5
(b) (4 + 5) x 6
(c) (3 x 5) + 6

A. (b)>(c)
B. (a)=(b)=(c)
C. (a)>(b) and (b)=(c)
D. (a)<(b) and (b)>(c)

25. What number is one third of the quantity 9 squared?

A. 81
B. 27
C. 64
D. 15

26. Examine the graph and find the best answer.

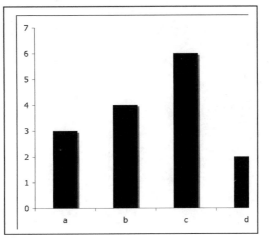

A. (c) minus (b) equals (b) minus (d)
B. (a) plus (d) equals (c)
C. (c) minus (d) equals (a)
D. (a) plus (b) equals (c) plus (d)

27. Examine the diagram of a circle and find the best answer. The chord shown is a diameter of the circle. The shorter line segment is a radius of the circle.

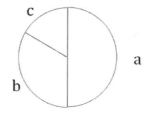

A. a = b = c
B. a>b and b< c
C. b = a – c
D. a + c = b

28. Examine (a), (b), and (c) and find the best answer.

(a) 5^2 (b) 2^5 (c) 25

A. (c)>(b)
B. (a)=(b)=(c)
C. (b)=(c)
D. (a)=(c) and (c)<(b)

29. Examine (a), (b), and (c) and find the best answer.

(a) A number that is 3 less than 2 times 15
(b) A number that is equal to 3 cubed
(c) A number that is 3 more than 80% of 30

A. (b)>(c)
B. (a)=(b)=(c)
C. (b)=(c)
D. (a)<(b) and (b)>(c)

30. If an odd number is added to an even number, the result must be

A. odd
B. even
C. positive
D. zero

31. Which of the following is equal to $4\sqrt{2^4}$?

A. 4
B. 8
C. 16
D. 32

32. A class contains an equal number of boys and girls. The average height of the boys is 62 inches. The average height of the all the students is 60 inches. What is the average height of the girls in the class?

    A. 57 inches

    B. 58 inches

    C. 59 inches

    D. 60 inches

33. A circle has an area equal to 36π. What is its diameter?

    A. 4

    B. 6

    C. 12

    D. 4π

34. Which of the following numerals is not a prime number?

    A. 3

    B. 6

    C. 17

    D. 41

35. A dartboard is divided into 8 black and 8 white wedge-shaped sectors, so that when a dart is thrown it has a 50% chance of landing on white, and a 50% chance of landing on black. If a dart is thrown 3 times in a row and lands on black each time, what is the chance that it will land again on black if it is thrown a fourth time?

12.5%

    A. 25%

    B. 50%

    C. 100%

36. How many integers exist between the numbers -4.2 and +6.1?

    A. 2

    B. 6

    C. 10

    D. 11

37. Which of the following must be true of a number x if $\sqrt{x} = \dfrac{1}{\sqrt{x}}$?

    A. $x = 0$

    B. $x = 1$

    C. $x = 2$

    D. x is negative

38. Which of the following expressions represents "five times a number m squared"?

    A. $\dfrac{5}{m^2}$

    B. $5m^2$

    C. $(5m)^2$

    D. $5 + m^2$

39. Juan got grades of 68 and 73 on his first two math tests. What grade must he get on the third test if all are weighted equally and he wants to raise his grade to a 75 average?

    A. 84
    B. 82
    C. 80
    D. 78

40. The ratio of left-handed to right-handed ballplayers on the girls' softball team is 2:3. If there are 12 left-handed players on the team, how many girls are on the roster in all?

    A. 18
    B. 24
    C. 30
    D. 32

41. The chart below represents the average amount of rain falling each month in the town of Tegulpa. During which month of the year does the most rain fall?

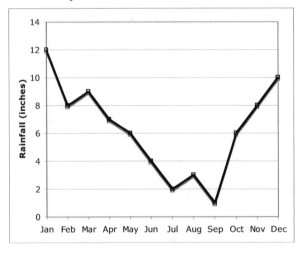

    A. January
    B. April
    C. August
    D. December

42. Refer to the chart shown with Question 23. Which month shows the greatest increase in rainfall compared to the preceding month?

    A. January
    B. March
    C. August
    D. October

43. Jamet had $6.50 in his wallet when he left home. He spent $4.25 on drinks and $2.00 on a magazine. Later, his friend repaid him $2.50 that he had borrowed the previous day. How much did Jamet have in his wallet then?

    A. $12.25
    B. $14.25
    C. $3.25
    D. $2.75

Question 44 is based upon the following table:

English-Metric Equivalents	
1 meter	1.094 yard
2.54 centimeter	1 inch
1 kilogram	2.205 pound
1 liter	1.06 quart

44. A sailboat is 19 meters long. What is its length in inches?

    A. 254

    B. 1,094

    C. 4,826

    D. 748

45. Mrs. Patterson's classroom has sixteen empty chairs in it. All the chairs are occupied when every student is present. If 2/5 of the students are absent, how many students make up her entire class?

    A. 16

    B. 32

    C. 24

    D. 40

46. Rachel spent $24.15 on vegetables. She bought 2 pounds of onions, 3 pounds of carrots, and $1\frac{1}{2}$ pounds of mushrooms. If the onions cost $3.69 per pound, and the carrots cost $4.29 per pound, what is the price per pound of mushrooms?

    A. $2.60

    B. $2.25

    C. $2.80

    D. $3.10

47. Lauren had $80 in her savings account. When she got her paycheck, she made a deposit that brought the total to $120. By what percentage did the total amount in her account increase as a result of this deposit?

    A. 50%

    B. 40%

    C. 35%

    D. 80%

48. An airplane leaves Atlanta at 2 PM and flies north at 250 miles per hour. A second airplane leaves Atlanta 30 minutes later and flies north at 280 miles per hour. At what time will the second airplane overtake the first?

    A. 6:00 PM

    B. 6:20 PM

    C. 6:40 PM

    D. 6:50 PM

49. A combination lock uses a 3-digit code. Each digit can be any one of the ten available integers 0-9. How many different combinations are possible?

    A. 9

    B. 1,000

    C. 81

    D. 100

50. In a row of airplane seats, three people are seated next to each other. Felix and Marta are a couple and must sit next to each other. How many different seating arrangements are possible?

    A. 2

    B. 4

    C. 6

    D. 8

Answer Key and Explanations

Language Answers

1. A: The use of the period before the word "When" suggests the start of a new sentence, but this actually creates a fragment. The comma sets off the dependent clause by creating a natural pause in the sentence.

2. D: No extra punctuation is necessary within the sentence. The conjunction "and" simply combines two verbs but not two independent clauses, or separate sentences, so no comma is necessary.

3. B: In this case, a comma is necessary before the conjunction "but," because this is a coordinating conjunction and joins two independent clauses, or separate sentences. Each independent clause has a unique subject-verb relationship, so the comma indicates that two separate ideas are being joined with a conjunction.

4. C: The word *us* makes the sentence grammatically correct. *Us* is the objective case of *we*. In this case, *us* is being used as an indirect object. An indirect object is the noun to which the action of the verb refers. In the sentence *He gave her a sandwich*, the indirect object is *her* (and the direct object is *sandwich*). All of the answer choices for this question are in the first-person plural, with the exception of answer choice D, which is in the third-person plural. The appropriate third-person plural form to complete this sentence is *them*.

5. A: The word *is* makes the sentence grammatically correct. In order to answer this question, you need to determine what the object of the verb will be. One way to do this is to rearrange the question as if it were a declarative sentence: *Picking up the groceries ____ one of the things you are supposed to do.* Expressed like this, it is easy to see that the subject of the sentence is "picking up the groceries." This is a third-person singular subject (that is, it is an "it"), so it receives the third-person present indicative verb form, *is*.

6. D: The word *our* makes the sentence grammatically correct. *Our* is the possessive case of *we*, In this case, *our* is being used as an attributive adjective. An adjective is a word that modifies (or describes) a noun. *Our* is called an attributive adjective because it is attributing (assigning) ownership of the screaming to a particular party, *us*. Answer choices A and D are in the first-person plural; answer choices B and C are in the third-person plural. Neither B nor C, however, is in the possessive case. The sentence could be effectively completed with *their*, but this choice is not available.

7. C: The longest word recorded in an English dictionary are "Pneumonoultramicroscopicsilicovolcanokoniosis."

    Error: Subject-verb disagreement

The subject of this sentence is the singular noun "word," so the plural verb "are" disagrees with the subject. The verb used here should be the singular "is."

8. B: The largest catfish ever catch is 646 pounds, the size of an adult brown bear.

    Error: Incorrect verb tense

The verb "catch" is not in the appropriate tense. It should be written in the past tense, "caught."

9. C: Though a highly influentially anthropologist, Claude Levi-Strauss often took criticism for spending little time in the field studying real cultures.

Error: Adverb / adjective error

The adverb "influentially" is being used to modify the noun "anthropologist." Since adverbs cannot modify nouns, "influentially" should be written in adjective form: "influential."

10. C: It is easy to get confused when calculating time differences between time zones a useful way to remember them is that the Atlantic Ocean starts with A, as in A.M., and the Pacific Ocean starts with P, as in P.M.

Error: Run-on sentence

Choice C contains two complete thoughts, each with its own subject and predicate. The second complete thought begins, "a useful way to remember them…." A sentence composed of two complete thoughts joined together without appropriate punctuation is called a "run-on." A period or semicolon should appear between the phrases "time zones" and "a useful way."

11. C: The surrealists were a group of artists who believed that art should reflect the subconscious mind, their images are often very dreamlike, showing businessmen falling like rain over a city and melting clocks.

Error: Comma splice

There are two complete sentences here joined by only a comma. A period or semicolon should replace the comma after "mind."

12. B: "Orange is my favorite color, but not my favorite fruit." said Lisa.

Error: Punctuation

The period that appears at the end of the quote should be a comma.

13. B: The deepest canyon, too.

Error: Fragment

This phrase contains a subject, but it does not contain a predicate, which makes it a sentence fragment.

14. A: Pocahontas spent the last year's of her young life in England under the name Rebecca.

Error: Apostrophe

The apostrophe in the word "year's" is unnecessary. The sentence should read, "Pocahontas spent the last years…."

15. A: The Pima Indians of Arizona have remarkably high rates of diabetes and obesity some scientists believe the gene that causes this present-day health crisis was actually of great value to the Pima's ancestors who had to be able to retain glucose during periods of famine.

Error: Run-on sentence

A sentence composed of two complete thoughts joined together without appropriate punctuation is called a "run-on." A period or semicolon should appear between "obesity" and "some scientists."

16. C: Director Alfred Hitchcock make over 60 films in his career.

Error: Subject-verb disagreement

The subject "Alfred Hitchcock" is a singular subject, which requires a singular verb. "Make" should be "makes."

17. D: No error.

18. D: This option is the simplest and most practical way to combine the two statements: one subject and two verbs developed from it. Answer choices A and B open with dependent clauses that make no sense in the context of the rest of the sentence. Answer choice C contains a coordinating conjunction that creates confusion between the first independent clause and the second.

19. A: Among the answer choices, option A combines the sentences in the smoothest way by adding the second sentence as an appositive phrase. Answer choice B fails to include the first sentence. Answer choice C makes little sense with the use of "because." Answer choice D reverses the sentences to combine them, but in doing so it does not make the sentences read any more effectively.

20. B: This option best indicates the sense of contrast between the statements. Answer choice A does not provide the contrast that is required to join the two sentences. Answer choice C makes little sense with the use of "Since" at the beginning of the sentence, and answer choice D is largely the same in failing to join the sentences with an effective transition.

21. D: The use of "After" at the beginning of the sentence combines the statements by creating a sense of chronology in Joseph Black's experiences. Answer choice A creates a contradiction that is inappropriate to the context of the sentences. Answer choice B could work, except that there is not enough in the first sentence to justify the need for "Because." Answer choice C is also incorrect, because the use of "Although" creates a contradiction that is not necessary.

22. B: Answer choice B offers the best topic sentence by providing a clear overview of the paragraph that follows. Answer choice A provides useful information but is too limited by attributing the Crusades solely to the "monarchs of Europe" (since the paragraph clearly indicates that the Crusades had a religious impetus as well). Answer choice C offers a sentence that belongs further in the paragraph by expressing detail rather than overview. Answer choice D provides interesting information, but this information has limited relevance to the specific material in the paragraph.

23. D: The use of "As a result" and "responded" provides a clear transition to explain what happened after the "Crusaders began massacring Muslim inhabitants and destroying Muslim religious centers." Answer choice A offers information that could potentially follow up the event, but it lacks the direct link from the event that answer choice D provides. Similarly, answer choice B fails to explain the link between the Christian destruction of Antioch and the need to join with Muslims in driving out Frankish mercenaries. Answer choice C is incorrect by reversing the chronology of the paragraph by describing events leading up to the fall of Antioch and then describing what happened before it.

- 41 -

24. A: The expression "Until then" moves the progress of thought from the end of the First Crusade and the beginning of the Second Crusade. Answer choice B offers the necessary in-between details, but they prove to be irrelevant to the rest of the paragraph. Answer choice C is also largely irrelevant to the paragraph as a whole. In the same way, answer choice D provides helpful information, but it is nonessential to the paragraph as a whole.

25. A: Answer choice A offers the clearest introduction to the topic of the paragraph, which is the start of the Third Crusade. Answer choice B provides a hint of this information but without the effective detail that answer choice A offers. Answer choice C places the focus on the leaders of the Third Crusade, instead of its beginning and successes, which is the focus of the paragraph. Answer choice D introduces Salāh ad-Dīn but gives him too much priority with reference to the rest of the paragraph.

26. C: Answer choice C effectively links the topic sentence with the final sentence, offering a clear description of how and why the schism occurred. Answer choice A is interesting but fails to provide a clear sense of wrapping up the paragraph. Answer choice B is an opinion statement about the events of the paragraph, rather than a statement concluding the paragraph, so it cannot be correct within the context. Answer choice D also verges on an opinion statement that is not appropriate to the context of the sentence, so it cannot be correct.

27. B: This option notes that the Fifth Crusade began with a Lateran Council that prepared for "two separate phases." As the rest of the paragraph describes these phrases and their effectiveness, answer choice B is the best transition from the topic sentence to the rest of the paragraph. Answer choice A places too much weight on the opinion of Pope Innocent III without offering a clear introduction of the phases. Answer choice C is more or less irrelevant as an introduction to the rest of the paragraph. Similarly, answer choice D introduces St. Francis of Assisi, but this proves to be largely unnecessary to the rest of the paragraph.

28. C: The explanation that Zosimos of Panapolis believed ancient Egyptian priests practiced alchemy follows most naturally from the statement that "the practice of alchemy is believed to date back to ancient Egypt." Answer choice A hints at this, but it does not provide the information as clearly as answer choice C does. Answer choice B verges widely from the topic, by pointing the focus in the direction of the Middle Ages. And answer choice D would be correct if the entire paragraph were about various parts of the world where the practice of alchemy occurred, but as the paragraph is about alchemy in ancient Egypt, answer choice D has no place.

29. D: The sentence notes that alchemists combined "scientific traditions, as well as religious and mystical beliefs." Answer choice D follows this up by noting two figures who fit into this description of traditions and beliefs. Answer choices A and B are largely irrelevant to the topic sentence and offer more confusion than clarity to the main idea. Answer choice C is distantly connected but might work better as a concluding statement for the paragraph than a follow-up statement to the topic sentence.

30. C: Sentence 4, regarding Jefferson's affair with one of his slaves, is not directly relevant to the main topic at hand, which is Jefferson's debts.

31. B: Sentence 2, regarding Feynman's musicianship, is of little relevance to the discussion of the atomic theory.

32. B: The phrase *to have extinction* in choice A is grammatically incorrect. In choice C, *causes* is plural, and so the word should be *exist* rather than *exists*. D is not the best choice because it is somewhat awkward. B sounds the best and is also grammatically correct.

33. C: Answer choice C is the best answer because it indicates a contrast and is grammatically correct.

34. A: Answer choice A is the best answer because it denotes the party to whom companies are offering tech support and because the verb *are* agrees with the noun *customers*.

35. D: Answer choice D is the best choice. The phrases *high-fat diets* and *excessive amounts of television* agree with each other because they are both plural. The word *is* refers to *the fact that*, so these also agree with each other.

36. B: This is a well-known phrase meaning *despite what most people believe*. The word *contrarily* in choice A makes it incorrect. *Popularity* in choice C is out of place, and *believing* in choice D is incorrect.

37. A: Answer choice B implies the Egyptians had long life spans, which doesn't make sense in the context of the sentence. Option C uses *its* instead of the grammatically correct *it's*, while D has misplaced commas and also uses *its*. Option A indicates the Egyptians lived a long time ago, and the correct form of *it's* is used.

38. B: The sentence describes a cause/effect relationship, so *because* is the correct way to begin the sentence. Choice A implies that technology changed in the past, which does not make sense in the context of the sentence. Option B indicates a cause/effect relationship, and states that technology is continuously changing, which is why IT professionals must continuously learn new skills.

39. D: D is the correct choice because the three verbs are in the same form. A and B use different verb forms. C is grammatically incorrect because of the *to* that is used to begin the sentence.

40. A: Saying that something can be *attributed to* something else is grammatically correct, which eliminates choices B and D. Option C is incorrect because *they* refers to antibiotics, so the sentence is essentially stating that antibiotics are prescribing. Inanimate objects are incapable of doing this, which makes the sentence incorrect. A states that antibiotics are prescribed, indicating someone else is doing the prescribing, which makes it the correct choice.

41. C: Option A is incorrect because *a* and *challenges* do not agree. Answer choice B is incorrect because *key challenge* must be prefaced by *a*. Choice D is incorrect because of the misplaced apostrophe, and also because the sentence only identifies one challenge, meaning the plural, *key challenges*, is incorrect.

42. D: Answer choice A is incorrect because *severely* is an adverb and not an adjective. Options B and C are incorrect because *problem* instead of the grammatically correct *problems* is used. Choice D uses the correct, plural form *problems* and uses adjectives to describe the problems.

43. A: The sentence implies that *velocity* is used to indicate more than one value, which eliminates choices B and D. The phrase refers to velocity, which is singular, but the construction of choice C would correctly refer to a plural noun. Choice A agrees with the singular, noun and the *and* indicates that velocity is used to indicate more than one value.

44. B: Answer choice B uses the grammatically correct *their* instead of *there*. The *to* indicates the companies are using these sites for something, and *services* and *products* agree with each other because they are both plural.

- 43 -

45. C: Answer choice C states that an autoclave is a tool used *to sterilize*. Choices A and B, which begin with *to sterilizing* and *for sterilize*, are not grammatically correct. Option D indicates that the machine is used to sterilize a single tool and needle, which does not make sense in the context of the sentence.

46. D: Answer choices A and C are incorrect because they imply that the bizarre creatures are something other than electric eels. The *a* in choice B does not agree with the plural *electric eels*. Choice D is best because it is grammatically correct and identifies electric eels as the bizarre creatures being discussed in the sentence.

47. A: Answer choice B is incorrect because the plural *key factors* and the singular *is* do not agree. The *taking* in choice C makes it incorrect. Choice D has a misplaced comma. Choice A makes sense and the singular *a key factor* and *is* agree with each other.

48. C: Choice C is the only choice that has correctly placed commas. The *numerous moons* and the *Great Red Spot* both refer to the planet Jupiter, which is maintained in answer choice C.

49. A: Answer choice B is incorrect because of the misplaced apostrophe. Answer choice C has two unnecessary commas. Answer choice D is too wordy, and *landfills wastes* sounds quite awkward. Answer choice A is succinct, the comma is in the correct place, and it expresses the information is a clear way that is not awkward.

50. D: Answer choices A and C are incorrect because *large* is used in front of *attributable* and *attributed.* Both of these phrases are grammatically incorrect. Option B describes *the growing of the securities industry*, which is quite awkward. Choice D is the best choice because it refers to *the growth of the security industry* and uses the phrase *largely attributed*, which is grammatically correct.

51. C: The correct way to refer to a person, in this case Monet, is through the use of the pronoun *whose*, which eliminates choices A and D. Two paintings are identified, so the plural form must be used, eliminating choice B. Option C uses *whose* and *paintings*, indicating there is more than one, making it the correct choice.

52. C: The original sentence is redundant and wordy.

53. C: The syntax of the original sentence is fine, but a comma after *said* but before the open-quotation mark is required.

54. D: In the original sentence, the modifier is placed too far away from the word it modifies.

Reading Skill Answers

1. D: The main idea of this passage is that vaccines help the immune system function properly. One of the common traps that many test-takers fall into is assuming that the first sentence of the passage will express the main idea. Although this will be true for some passages, often the author will use the first sentence to attract interest or to make an introductory, but not central, point. On this question, if you assume that the first sentence contains the main idea, you will mistakenly choose answer B. Finding the main idea of a passage requires patience and thoroughness; you cannot expect to know the main idea until you have read the entire passage. In this case, a diligent reading will show you that answer choices A, B, and C express details from the passage, but only answer choice D is a comprehensive summary of the author's message.

2. C: This passage does not state that the symptoms of disease will not emerge until the body has learned to fight the disease. In this question, the details expressed in answer choices A, B, and D are all explicit in the passage. The passage never states, however, that the symptoms of disease do not emerge until the body has learned how to fight the disease-causing microbe. On the contrary, the passage implies that a person may become quite sick and even die before the body learns to effectively fight the disease.

3. B: In the third paragraph, the word *virulent* means "malicious." In some cases, you may already know the basic definition of the word. Nevertheless, you should always go back and look at the way the word is used in the passage. The exam may include answer choices that are legitimate definitions for the given word, but which do not express how the word is used in the passage. For instance, the word *virulent* could in some circumstances mean contagious or annoying. However, since the passage is not talking about transfer of the disease and is referring to a serious illness, malicious is the more appropriate answer.

4. C: The author's primary purpose in writing this essay is to inform. If the passage took an objective look at the pros and cons of various approaches to fighting disease, we would say that the passage was a piece of analysis. Because the purpose of this passage is to present new information to the reader in an objective manner, however, it is clear that the author's intention is to inform.

5. D: Lisa and Regina are the only pair whose ads *both* advised that they would be available for weekend childcare.

6. C: Regina and Jose are the only pair whose ads both advised that they were available for occasional childcare.

7. D: No one but Regina fits the family's needs. Lisa will only watch 3 kids, James wants full-time work, and Jose is only available for occasional babysitting.

8. C: James' ad notes that he would consider cooking in addition to childcare.

9. B: We can infer Jose is the youngest from the information in his ad that he is a high-school junior.

10. B: Accessories decreased by 14%, a higher decrease than any of the other departments.

11. D: Overall sales were lowest in every department in the 4th Quarter 2008.

12. A: Women's wear sales were at 157 in 1st Quarter 2008 and returned to 157 in the 1st Quarter 2009.

13. C: The ad notes in the second sentence that candidates must be members of the California State Bar Association.

14. C: "Competitive salary" means on that is similar to the average offered for comparable jobs.

15. A: Since the ad suggests that candidates should be able to work in a self-directed capacity and as part of a team, it can be inferred that they might have both those work experiences.

16. B: The California Update notes state that the upcoming election will be discussed.

17. A: Smart Talk and Car Talk note that they are call-in shows

18. C: Smart Talk lists a discussion about President Obama's first 100 days in office.

19. B: The environment will most likely be discussed most in a program on green jobs.

20. D: This statement is most likely to be made in a show on graffiti.

21. C: The 8:20 would get you in at 8:33. The next latest, the 8:35, would get you in too late at 8:48.

22. C: The train makes three stops: South Hayward, Hayward, and Bay Fair.

23. A: From Union City to South Hayward is 5 minutes; all others are 4 minutes.

24. D: From Hayward to Bay Fair is 4 minutes and the shortest trip.

25. D: The 8:30 train would get you there at 8:44.

26. A: The Fremont to Union City trip takes 5 minutes; all others take 4 minutes.

27. D: The third sentence notes that concern over mainstream media portrayal of homelessness was partly the reason for the emergence of the papers.

28. B: The first sentence of the passage notes that these papers are primarily sold by homeless people.

29. C: The vendors net the list price for which they sell the paper minus the percentage they pay of the list price.

30. B: Hunter Gatherer is not a name the passage gives for a diet.

31. B: Dairy is listed as a food that is not allowed on the diet.

32. A: The passage notes that the idea behind the diet is that we are genetically adapted to the diet of our Paleolithic forebears.

33. B: The last sentence of the passage states that some studies support the idea of positive health benefits from the diet.

34. D: The second sentence describes the balance sought.

35. A: This is stated in the fourth sentence.

36. B: The context implies this is a good way to decide upon activities at which the child will be happy.

37. D: This is stated in the fifth sentence.

38. C: Choice C is the best answer. The sentence reads, "Your brain <u>filters</u> [your nose] out," which means your brain ignores it.

39. B: Only choice B reflects the meaning of the term "retina," which is a part of the eye's anatomy.

40. B: The final sentence reads, "Your brain works hard to make the world look continuous." It follows that visual perception is an active process, not a passive one, making choice B the best answer.

41. A: If the reader follows the instructions given in the paragraph, the O and X in the middle of the passage can be used to demonstrate the blind spot in the visual field. Choice A is the best answer.

- 46 -

42. B: The passage explains the way that visual perception works. Choice B is the best answer.

43. D: Much of the information in the passage is provided to show examples of how the brain fills in gaps in the visual field. Choice D is the best answer.

44. A: The author of the passage mentions the nose to demonstrate how the brain filters information out of the visual field. Choice A is the best answer.

Mathematics Computation Answers

1. D: This is a simple addition problem with carrying. Start with the ones column and add 6+4, write down the 0 and add the 1 to the digits in the tens column. Now add 9+0+1. Write down the 0 and add the 1 to the digits in the hundreds column. Now add 3+7+1 and write down the 1. Add the 1 to the thousands column. Add 3+2+1 and write the 6 to get the answer: 6100.

2. B: This is a simple subtraction problem. Start with the ones column and subtract 7-6, then 3-1, then 5-3, then 8-6 to get 2,221.

3. C: This is a multiplication problem with carrying. Start with the ones column. Multiply 2 by each digit above it beginning with the ones column. Write down each product: going across-- it will read 1268. Now multiply 7 by each of the digits above it. Write down each product: going across, the figure will read 4501. Ensure that the 1 is in the tens column and the other numbers fall evenly to the right. Now add the numbers like a regular addition problem to get 46,296.

4. C: This is a multiplication problem with 0. Start with the 4 and multiply it by each of the digits at the top. 6 x 4 is 24. Write down the 4 and place the 2 in the tens column. 0 x 4 is 0. Add the 2. 8 x 4 is 32. The top line will read 3224. Now add a 0 at the end of the next line, and then multiply 3 by 6. Write down the 8 and place the 1 in the tens column. 0 x 3 is 0. Add the 1. 8 x 3 is 24. The bottom line will read 24180. Add these together, and the answer will be 27,404.

5. B: This is a simple division problem. Divide the 5 into 8. It goes in 1 time. Write 1 above the 8 and subtract 5 from 8 to get 3. Bring down the 5 and place it beside the 3. Divide 5 into 35. It goes in 7 times. Divide 5 into 4. It goes 0 times. There is 4 remaining.

6. D: This is a simple division problem. Divide 63 into 181. It goes in 2 times. Write 2 above the 1 and subtract 126 from 181. The result is 55. Bring down the 4. Divide 63 in 554. It goes in 8 times. Write 8 above the first 4 and subtract 504 from 554 to get 50. Bring down the 4. Divide 63 into 504. It goes in 8 times.

7. B: To change this fraction into a decimal, divide 1000 into 72.000. 1000 goes into 72.00 7 times. Ensure that the decimal and 0 come before the 7.

8. D: This is multiplication with decimals. Multiply 3 by 9 to get 27. Put down the 7 and carry the 2. Multiply 3 by 1 to get 3. Add the 2. Write 5 to the left of 5. Multiply the 2 by the 9 to get 18. Enter the 8 and carry 1. Multiply 2 by 1 to get 2. Add 1 and write down 3. Add the two lines together, making sure that the 8 in the bottom figure is even with the 5. Get 437. Count 4 decimal points over (2 from the top multiplier and 2 from the second multiplier) and add a 0 before adding the decimal.

9. C: To solve, divide .08 into .3. Move the decimal in .08 over 2 places to make it an 8. Because this decimal point was moved 2 places, it must be done to the other decimal too. .3 becomes 30.0. Now divide 8 into 30. Put a 3 above 0 (ensure that the decimal is beside it) and subtract 24 from 30.

- 47 -

Bring down the 0 and put it beside the 6. Divide 8 into 60. Put 7 above the 0 and subtract 56 from 60. Bring down the 0 and put it beside the 4. Divide 8 into 40. Put 5 beside the 7.

10. A: This is a simple subtraction problem involving decimals. Line up the decimals and subtract 7 from 3. Since 7 is a larger number than 3, borrow ten from the 4. Cross out the 4 and make it 3. Now subtract 7 from 13 to get 6. Subtract 1 from 3 and get 2. Place the decimal point before the 2.

11. A: To add fractions, ensure that the denominator (the number on the bottom) is always the same common denominator. Since there is not common denominator in this case, change both fractions to 14ths. 1/2 equals 7/14. 1/7 equals 2/14. Now add the whole numbers: 2+3 = 5 and the resulting fraction become 9/14.

12. B: To subtract fractions, ensure that the denominator (the number on the bottom) is the same. Having the same "common denominator" is essential to solving the problem. Since there is no common denominator in this case, t, change both fractions to 36ths. 1/9 equals 4/36. 1/4 equals 9/36. The equation now looks like this: $3\frac{4}{36} - 1\frac{9}{36}$. Change the 3 to 2 and add 36 to the numerator (the top number) so that the fractions can be subtracted. The equation now looks like this: $2\frac{40}{36} - 1\frac{9}{36} = 1\frac{31}{36}$

13. A: To multiply mixed numbers, you must first create improper fractions. Multiply the whole number by the denominator, and then add the numerator.

$$3\frac{1}{8} \text{ becomes } \frac{25}{8}$$

The problem will look like this: $\frac{25}{8} \times \frac{19}{3} \times \frac{12}{5} = \frac{5700}{120} = 47\frac{1}{2}$

14. A: To divide fractions, change the second fraction to its reciprocal (its reverse) and multiply: $\frac{1}{8} \times \frac{5}{4}$

15. B: To solve, test each answer. Notice that in (A), the numerator has been multiplied by 9 to get 18. The denominator has been multiplied by 8. These are not equal fractions. In (C) the numerator has been multiplied by 4 and the denominator has been multiplied by 2. These are not equal fractions. In (D) the numerator has been multiplied by 3 and the denominator has been multiplied by 2. These are not equal fractions. In (B), both numerator and denominator have been multiplied by 4.

16. B: The denominator has been multiplied by 4 to get 20. Think of what number multiplied by 4 totals 12.

17. C: Divide the numerator and denominator by 17.

18. A: Since all the answers have a 7 as the whole number, multiply 7 x 14. The answer is 98. The remainder is 1.

19. A: 10% of 900 is 90. Multiply 90 by 3 to find 30%.

20. A: Divide 2 by 40 to get .05 or 5%

21. C: Divide 60 by 5 to get 12. Multiply 12 by 3.

22. C: Rewrite the problem as $40 \times .5\%$ and solve.

23. A: Divide 2 by 10 (not 10 by 2)

24. D: To solve, first get both fractions on the same side of the equation to isolate the percentage sign. When $\frac{3}{4}$ is moved to the opposite side of the equation, it must be divided by the fraction there:
$$\frac{3}{10} \div \frac{3}{4}$$

To divide one fraction into another, multiply by the reciprocal of the denominator:
$$\frac{3}{10} \times \frac{4}{3} = \frac{12}{30} = \frac{2}{5} = 40\%$$

25. B: To change a fraction to a percent, multiply it by 100:
$$\frac{36}{9} \times \frac{100}{1}$$

26. D: To solve, divide 25 into 4.

27. A: To solve, first write the fraction as $\frac{15}{100}$. Reduce by dividing numerator and denominator both by 5.

28. A: To change a percent to a decimal, remove the percent sign and move the decimal two spaces to the left.

29. C: It is quickest to find 30% of each answer given. (A): 10% of 90 is 9, so 30% is 27. (B): 10% of 180 is 18, so 30% is 54. (C): 10% of 200 is 20, so 30% is 60. (D): 10% of 210 is 21, so 30% is 63.

30. B: To solve change 1 ¼% to a decimal: .0125. Now add an x for the question mark:
$.0125x = 1.5$. Divide 1.5 by .0125.

31. C: To solve, rewrite the equation with a decimal in place of the percent:
$$8 = .25x$$
$$x = \frac{8}{.25} = \frac{800}{25} = 32$$

32. C: To solve, change the percent to a decimal:
$$.40x = 18$$
$$x = \frac{18}{.40} = \frac{1800}{40} = 45$$

33. B: To solve, add 4a and 5a, then subtract 7a.

34. C: To solve, combine like terms, ensuring that the subtraction sign is noted and positive/negative signs are changed accordingly: $x^2 - x^2 = 0$; 2x – 3x = -x; 2 – 6 = -4

35. B: To solve, get the variable (y) by itself:

$$3y = 30 - 6; 3y = 24; y = 8$$

36. A: To solve, first do the multiplication on each side of the equation:

$5x + 10 = 3x + 12$. Then get like terms on opposite sides of the equation: $2x = 2; x = 1$

37. B: Since they are like terms, just subtract.

38. C: To solve, first do the operations in parenthesis, then add like terms:

$$7x + 21 - 3 + 3x + 3 = 10x + 21$$

39. C: To solve, get like terms on opposite sides of the equation:

$$3x = 21; x = 7$$

40. D: To solve, first do the operations in parenthesis, then add/subtract like terms. The final step is to get like terms on the appropriate sides of the equation:

$$2r + 6 + 2 = 3r + 18$$

Applied Mathematics Answers

1. A: Convert all the numbers to fractions and compare. The number 0.099 can be rounded to 0.1. Then, the first 3 choices are: a) 1/3; b) 1/4; c) 1/100. Since the numerators are equal, the number with the smallest denominator is greatest, and that is 1/3. To compare that with choice D, note that 1/3 = 2/6 and 2/6 > 2/7.

2. C: The difference 27 – 23 = 4, and 300% of 4 is 3 times 4, or 12.

3. A: Each element of the series adds 9 to the preceding one. In algebraic terms, $P_n = P_{n-1} + 9$, where P_n is the nth element of the series. Since 31 + 9 = 40, 40 is the correct answer.

4. B: To compute the average, first find the sum of all the items in the list and then divide by the number of items in the list. This yields $\dfrac{3+4+5}{3} = \dfrac{12}{3} = 4$. One half of 4 is 2.

5. D: Since the line segments pass through the center of the circle, both $\overline{AB}$ and $\overline{CD}$ are diameters of equal length, and the four line segments radiating outwards from O are all equal-length radii.

6. A: Since 20% is equivalent to 1/5, it will take 5 times as long to download the entire piece of music. 5 x 15 = 75 minutes, this is equivalent to 1 hour 15 minutes.

7. D: Since the airplane is moving against a headwind, it will be slowed relative to the ground. Therefore its final speed will be 300 mph – 15 mph = 285 mph.

8. C: The average is computed by dividing the sum of all the measurements by the number of measurements. Let B = the average height of the boys, G = the average height of the girls, and C = the average height of the class. Since the number of boys and the number girls are equal, then $(B + G)/2$ = C. Then $B + G = 2C$. Substituting the known values, 110 + G = 2 x 105 and 110 + G = 210. Subtracting 110 from each side of the equation, G = 100.

9. C: Multiply both the numerator and denominator of fraction (a) by 10 to convert to the same denominator as the other two fractions. Then compare the numerators: $\dfrac{30}{50} < \dfrac{40}{50} > \dfrac{8}{50}$.

10. D: Since $4^3 = 4 \times 4 \times 4 = 64$, and $3^4 = 3 \times 3 \times 3 \times 3 = 81$, the answer is $81 - 64 = 17$.

11. B: The series consists of numbers each of which is double the number preceding. The number prior to the blank is 4: $2 \times 4 = 8$. The number following the blank is 16: $2 \times 8 = 16$.

12. C: Each section represents one fourth of the circle. Although the shaded areas in (a), (b), and (c) are oriented differently, each of them represents two quadrants, or half the area of the circle. The shaded area in (d) is only a single quadrant.

13. C: A number raised to the first power is multiplied by itself only once, so $16^1 = 16$. 2^8 is 2 multiplied by itself eight times, so $2^8 = 256$. Similarly, $3^3 = 27$.

14. A: The series alternates between subtracting 4 from the number occurring two positions earlier (12, 8, 4, 0) and adding 6 to the number occurring two positions earlier (7, 13, 19, 25). Therefore, 25 is the next number.

15. B: .20% of 80 = 16; 50% of 70 = 35; and 40% of 90 = 36. Since 36 > 35 > 16, B is correct.

16. C: Since $3^2 = 9$, and $3 \times 9 = 27$, C is correct.

17. A: Since $\dfrac{4 \times 30}{5} = \dfrac{120}{5} = 24$, and $24 + 3 = 27$, A is correct.

18. A: The sum $3 + 4 + 16 = 23$. The other choices are less. In particular, although it has more terms, choice B, $6 + 4 + 5 + 7 = 22$, which is less than choice A.

19. A: The numbers defined by (a), (b), and (c) are (a) 8; (b) 6; and (c) 15, respectively, so that choice A is correct.

20. C: The perimeter of a rectangle of length 6 and width 4 equals $2(6 + 4) = 20$. The perimeter of a square of side 4 equals $4 + 4 + 4 + 4 = 16$. And the area of a square of side 4 equals $4 \times 4 = 16$. Although the units for the measurement of area differ from those of the perimeters, the magnitude of the measurements for (b) and (c) are the same.

21. B: To compute the average, first total all the items in the list and then divide by the number of items in the list. This yields $\dfrac{20 + 35 + 45 + 20}{4} = \dfrac{120}{4} = 30$. The difference between 45 and 30 is 15.

22. C: The mean of a set of numbers equals their sum divided by the number of items in the set. Since there are three numbers in all, their sum must be 33 for the mean to compute to 11 (i.e., 33/3 = 11). Since $8 + 13 = 21$, the third number must be 12, since $33 - 12 = 21$.

23. B: Fractions can be simplified by dividing both numerator and denominator by the same number. Divide the numerator and denominator of item (b) by 10, and the result is 2/3. Divide the numerator and denominator of (c) by 15, and the result is 2/3. Therefore, all three fractions are equal.

24. D: Following normal order of operations, the expressions within the parentheses must be evaluated first. Expression (a), $(3 \times 4) + 5 = 12 + 5 = 17$. Expression (b), $(4+5) \times 6 = 9 \times 6 = 54$. Expression (c), $(3 \times 5) + 6 = 15 + 6 = 21$.

25. B: A number squared is that number multiplied by itself, so that 9 squared is $9^2 = 81$. Since one third of 81 equals 27, B is correct.

26. A: Read the values of each bar from the vertical axis: (a) = 3; (b) = 4; (c) = 6; and (d) = 2. Since 6 – 4 = 2, and 4 – 2 = 2, choice A is correct.

27. C: The straight line separating section (a) from sections (b) and (c) is a diameter. Therefore, section (a) is equal to one half of the circle. Since (b) and (c) together make up the remaining half of the circle, their sum is equal to section (a). Since b + c = a, it follows that b = a – c.

28. D: 5 squared is equal to 5 x 5 = 25, so that (a) is equal to (c). However, 2^5 = 2 x 2 x 2 x 2 x 2 = 32, so that (b) is greater than (a) or (c).

29. B: (a) 2 x 15 = 30 and 30 – 3 = 27; (b) 3^3 = 3 x 3 x 3 = 27; (c) $\dfrac{80 \times 30}{100} = 24$, and 24 + 3 = 27. Therefore, all three expressions are equal to 27.

30. A: An odd number can be considered as an even number N plus 1. Two even numbers added together produce an even number, so the result of adding an odd and an even number must be an even number plus 1, which is odd. For example, 4 + 3 = 7.

31. C: The square root of a number which is raised to the 4th power is the same number raised to the 2nd power. That is, $\sqrt{2^4} = 2^2 = 4$. Since 4 x 4 = 16, C is correct.

32. B: The average, or arithmetic mean, is computed by totaling all the measurements and dividing by the number of measurements. Let T_B represent the sum of the heights of the boys in the class, and T_G the sum of the heights of the girls. If N is the number of students in the class, there are $N/2$ boys and $N/2$ girls. The average height of the boys is then $\dfrac{T_B}{\dfrac{N}{2}} = \dfrac{2T_B}{N} = 62$. Similarly, the average

height of the girls is $\dfrac{2T_G}{N}$. The average height of all the students is equal to $\dfrac{T_B + T_G}{N} = \dfrac{T_B}{N} + \dfrac{T_G}{N} = 60$.

Therefore, $\dfrac{T_G}{N} = 60 - \dfrac{T_B}{N} = 60 - 31 = 29$, and the average height for the girls is 2 x 29 = 58.

33. C: The area of a circle is equal to πr², where r is the radius. Therefore, $\pi r^2 = 36\pi$, and $r = \sqrt{36} = 6$. Since the diameter is two times the radius, it is equal to 12.

34. B: A prime number has only two whole integer divisors, 1 and itself. This is true of 3, 17, and 41. However 6 can be divided by 1, 2, 3, and 6. It is therefore not a prime number.

35. C: Each throw of the dart is an independent event, and has no influence on the outcome of any other throw. Every time the dart is thrown, it has a 50% chance of landing on black, irrespective of the results of previous throws.

36. D: The integers are -4, -3, -2, -1, 0, +1, +2, +3, +4, +5, and +6.

37. B: Since $\sqrt{1} = 1$, then $\frac{1}{\sqrt{1}} = 1$. Note that $\sqrt{0} = 0$, so choice A results in an undefined number, since one cannot divide by zero. In addition, since one cannot have the square root of a negative number, choice D is incorrect.

38. B: The verbal description "five times a number m squared" means that m must be squared, and the resulting number multiplied by 5. Choice C is incorrect because the value within the parentheses is evaluated first, so that both 5 and m are squared. This results in a value of $25m^2$, which is incorrect.

39. A: The average, or arithmetic mean, is computed by totaling all the measurements and dividing by the number of measurements. To obtain an average of 75 from 3 measurements, the measurements must total 3 x 75 = 225. Since 68 + 73 = 141, then 225 – 141 = 84 points are required on the third test.

40. C: The ratio of left- to right-handed players will be the same as the ratio 2:3. Therefore, $\frac{2}{3} = \frac{12}{R}$, so that $R = 18$ right-handed players. The total number on the roster is therefore 12 + 18 = 30.

41. A: The graph is at its highest point for the first data point, which corresponds to 12 inches of rain during the month of January.

42. D: Rainfall in October increases to 6 inches, from 1 inch in September. This represents an increase of 5 inches. None of the other month-to-month differences are as great.

43. D: Jamet had $2.75 after all the transactions described. To solve this problem, first subtract $4.25 and then $2.00 from the initial sum of $6.50, leaving $0.25. Then add $2.50, arriving at the final answer of $2.75.

44. D: There are two ways to solve this problem: either convert meters to centimeters and then use the conversion factor in the table to convert centimeters to inches, or else use the table to convert meters to yards, and then convert to inches.

In the first instance, recall that there are 100 centimeters in a meter (*centi* means "hundredth"). Therefore $19m = 1{,}900\,cm = (\frac{1{,}900}{2.54}) = 748$ inches.

In the second instance, recall that there are 36 inches in a yard, therefore $19m = 19 \times 1.094 = 20.786\,yd = 20.786 \times 36 = 748$ inches.

45. D: Since 16 chairs are empty, and this represents 2/5 of the total enrollment, then the full class must consist of

$$\text{Class} = \frac{5}{2} \times 16 = 40 \text{ students}$$

46. A: To answer this question, we first determine the total cost of the onions and carrots, since these prices are given. This will equal (2 x $3.69 + 3 x $4.29) = $20.25. Next, this sum is subtracted from the total cost of the vegetables to determine the cost of the mushrooms: $24.15 - $20.25 =

$3.90. Finally, the cost of the mushrooms is divided by the quantity in lbs to determine the cost per lb:

$$\text{Cost per lb} = \frac{\$3.90}{1.5} = \$2.60$$

47. A: The percentage of increase equals the change in the account balance divided by the original amount, $80, and multiplied by 100. First, determine the change in the balance by subtracting the original amount from the new balance: $Change = \$120 - \$80 = \$40$. Now, determine the percentage of increase as described above: $Percent = \dfrac{\$40}{\$80} \times 100 = 50\%$.

48. C: Define a variable t as the elapsed time in minutes from the time the first airplane takes off. Then at any time the distance traveled by the first plane is $d_1 = 250t$. The second plane takes off 30 minutes later, so at any time the distance that it has traveled is $d_2 = 280(t - 30)$. This plane will overtake the first when the two distances are equal, that is when $d_1 = d_2$, or when $250t = 280(t - 30)$. Solve this last equation for t. First use the distributive property: $250t = 280t - 30 \times 280 = 280t - 8400$

Next, add 8,400 to each side of the equation: $250t + 8400 = 280t$

Next, subtract $250t$ from each side of the equation: $8400 = 30t$

Next, divide both sides by 30: $280 = t$.

This gives the value of t in minutes. Convert to hours by dividing 280 by 60 minutes per hour, which yields an elapsed time of 4 hours and 40 minutes. Since the first plane left at 2 PM, 4 hours and 40 minutes later is 6:40 PM.

49. B: In this probability problem there are three independent events (the codes for each digit), each with ten possible outcomes (the numerals 0-9). Since the events are independent, the total possible outcomes equals the product of the possible outcomes for each of the three events, that is $P = P_1 \times P_2 \times P_3 = 10 \times 10 \times 10 = 1{,}000$

50. B: Fred and Marta may be seated on the left or the right, which yields two combinations. Within each of these arrangements, Fred may sit to the right of Marta or to her left. Therefore, the total number of seating arrangements is 2 x 2 = 4 possible combinations.

Practice Test #2

Language Practice Questions

For Questions 1-3, select the correct punctuation mark for the sentence.

1. It turns out that the wildly popular multicolored tulips were suffering from a type of virus the tulip breaking virus that gives tulips a speckled appearance.

    A. :
    B. ;
    C. ,
    D. None

2. The Dutch created a trading market for tulip bulbs resembling the modern-day market for the sales of stocks futures and contracts.

    A. ,
    B. .
    C. :
    D. None

3. Tulip prices continued to climb on the Dutch tulip market until February of 1637 there were no bids on tulips one day, and the market collapsed completely.

    A. !
    B. .
    C. ,
    D. None

For Questions 4-6, choose the best word or phrase to complete the sentence.

4. Why did we _____ try so hard?

    A. has to
    B. haven't
    C. had to
    D. have to

5. Tracey wore her hair in a French braid, _____ was the style at the time.

    A. among
    B. it
    C. that
    D. which

6. The other day, Stan _____ reviewing his class notes in preparation for the final exam.

    A. begins
    B. begun
    C. begin
    D. began

For Questions 7-17, identify the sentence that contains an error in usage, punctuation or grammar. If there are no errors, choose answer choice "D."

7.

    A. The earliest recording of a human voice was made by Thomas Edison in 1877, when they recorded himself reciting "Mary Had a Little Lamb."
    B. In 2009, *The Simpsons* became the longest running series in television history.
    C. Many say that Reunion Tower in downtown Dallas, Texas, resembles a microphone or a golf ball on a tee.
    D. No mistake.

8.

    A. The *trireme* was a Greek battleship that got its name from the three banks of oars that helped propel the ship into battle.
    B. Our basement floods once a yearly.
    C. The *novitiate* is the period of time before a monk or priest takes his vows to make sure he is suited for the religious life.
    D. No mistake.

9.

    A. The trumpet player said, "I played the song right, just not the notes."
    B. Woody Allen said, "I don't want to achieve immortality through my work. I want to achieve it through not dying."
    C. Samuel Goldwyn is said to have replied to a secretary who asked whether she should destroy files over ten years old, "Yes, but keep copies."
    D. No mistake.

10.

    A. When asked to take a reduction in pay from $20,000 to $7,500 a year, baseball legend Vernon Gomez replied, "You keep the salary and pay me the cut."
    B. The spread of Islam began around 600 A.D. and reached from the Middle East to North Africa, Spain, Central Asia, and India?
    C. Hadrian, Emperor of Rome, is credited with halting the expansion of the Roman Empire to concentrate instead on defending its boundaries.
    D. No mistake.

11.

    A. The Sahara Desert was rarely crossed until the introduction of the camel in 100 A.D.
    B. International time standards were not put in place until 1883.
    C. The names of the days of the week originate in either Latin or Saxon names for deities Sunday, for instance, is Saxon for "Sun's Day," while Thursday derives from "Thor's Day."
    D. No mistake.

12.

A. The origin of the clock is usually traced back to Galileo, who in 1583 reportedly watched a chandelier swinging during a church service and imagined a way to use a pendulum as a time-keeping device.
B. Irvin Hertzel ran a statistical analysis of Monopoly squares and found that players land on some spots more often than others, specifically Illinois Ave., Go, B & O Railroad, and Free Parking.
C. Held in Georgia, the Masters is an annual golf tournament that professional golfers consider the most valuable title in golf.
D. No mistake.

13.

A. Ironically, the namesake of the Nobel Peace Prize, Alfred Nobel, are most noted for his invention of dynamite in the 1860s.
B. The terms of our lease agreement were long and hard to understand.
C. Many terms in our legal system are Latin in origin, such as "nolo contendere" (no contest) and "actus rea" (a wrongful act).
D. No mistake.

14.

A. Loud sounds can causing damage to the hair cells that turn sound waves into electrical signals that the brain perceives as sound.
B. Debate has raged for over 200 years about whether the U.S. should adopt the metric system.
C. The metric system recognizes only seven base units of measurement, including the meter for length, the kilogram for mass, and lesser known units used by specialists like the mole for substance and the candela for light intensity.
D. No mistake.

15.

A. The metric system uses a "base-ten" system of measurement, which means its prefixes indicate multiples of ten.
B. If you ever need to measure something but do not have access to a ruler, these facts can help: The average credit card is $3\frac{3}{8}$ inches by $2\frac{1}{8}$ inches, the diameter of a quarter is around one inch, and the diameter of a penny is about $\frac{3}{4}$ inch.
C. Carbon monoxide Poisoning can cause disorientation and delirium, and it can induce a coma.
D. No mistake.

16.

A. Capgras Syndrome causes the strange delusion that people such as family members and friends are not who they appear to be but are instead imposters.
B. Yvette belonged to three organizations whose schedules constantly conflicted.
C. Owen's shirt was stained pink from his popsicle, purple from jelly, and blue from Kool-Aid.
D. No mistake.

17.

A. They closed the parking deck at midnight, so we could not get no cars out until morning.
B. "Associationism" is the name given to the theory that memories are linked together so that when one is triggered, associated memories are activated as well.
C. Some psychologists believe that many emotional disorders, including depression and anxiety, can be traced back to unrealistic expectations and assumptions.
D. No mistake.

For Questions 18-21, select the answer that best combines the underlined sentences into one.

18. Adam Ferguson studied in the fields of history and philosophy. It was his work in exploring society and man's place in society that earned him the nickname "father of sociology."

A. While Adam Ferguson studied in the fields of history and philosophy, it was his work in exploring society and man's place in society that earned him the nickname "father of sociology."
B. Adam Ferguson studied in the fields of history and philosophy, and it was his work in exploring society and man's place in society that earned him the nickname "father of sociology."
C. When Adam Ferguson studied in the fields of history and philosophy, it was his work in exploring society and man's place in society that earned him the nickname "father of sociology."
D. Adam Ferguson studied in the fields of history and philosophy; it was his work in exploring society and man's place in society that earned him the nickname "father of sociology."

19. Novelist Sir Walter Scott is remembered for his contribution to Scottish literature. His most famous novels include *Rob Roy*, *The Bride of Lammermoor*, and *Ivanhoe*.

A. Because novelist Sir Walter Scott is remembered for his contribution to Scottish literature, his most famous novels include *Rob Roy*, *The Bride of Lammermoor*, and *Ivanhoe*.
B. Novelist Sir Walter Scott is remembered for his contribution to Scottish literature, but his most famous novels include *Rob Roy*, *The Bride of Lammermoor*, and *Ivanhoe*.
C. Novelist Sir Walter Scott is remembered for his contribution to Scottish literature: his most famous novels include *Rob Roy*, *The Bride of Lammermoor*, and *Ivanhoe*.
D. While Novelist Sir Walter Scott is remembered for his contribution to Scottish literature, his most famous novels include *Rob Roy*, *The Bride of Lammermoor*, and *Ivanhoe*.

20. Moral philosopher Adam Smith brought new ideas to the Scottish Enlightenment with his economic treatise *Wealth of Nations*. This book had far-reaching effects and ultimately impacted the American movement for independence.

A. Although moral philosopher Adam Smith brought new ideas to the Scottish Enlightenment with his economic treatise *Wealth of Nations*, this book had far-reaching effects and ultimately impacted the American movement for independence.
B. Moral philosopher Adam Smith brought new ideas to the Scottish Enlightenment with his economic treatise *Wealth of Nations*, a book that had far-reaching effects and ultimately impacted the American movement for independence.
C. Since moral philosopher Adam Smith brought new ideas to the Scottish Enlightenment with his economic treatise *Wealth of Nations*, this book had far-reaching effects and ultimately impacted the American movement for independence.
D. Moral philosopher Adam Smith brought new ideas to the Scottish Enlightenment with his economic treatise *Wealth of Nations*, but this book had far-reaching effects and ultimately impacted the American movement for independence.

21. James Watt's experiments in mechanical engineering resulted in a more effective steam engine. Today he is remembered for inventing the idea of horsepower and giving his name to the unit of power known as the "watt."

    A. James Watt's experiments in mechanical engineering resulted in a more effective steam engine, but today he is remembered for inventing the idea of horsepower and giving his name to the unit of power known as the "watt."

    B. James Watt's experiments in mechanical engineering resulted in a more effective steam engine, and today he is remembered for inventing the idea of horsepower and giving his name to the unit of power known as the "watt."

    C. After James Watt's experiments in mechanical engineering resulted in a more effective steam engine, today he is remembered for inventing the idea of horsepower and giving his name to the unit of power known as the "watt."

    D. James Watt's experiments in mechanical engineering resulted in a more effective steam engine: today he is remembered for inventing the idea of horsepower and giving his name to the unit of power known as the "watt."

For Questions 22-27, choose the best sentence to fill in the blank in the paragraph.

22. The Sixth Crusade was headed by Holy Roman Emperor Frederick II, who launched a crusade in 1228 to incur penance for his procrastination. Frederick had promised for some time that he would lead a crusade, but he continued to disappoint by failing to take action. An irritated Pope Gregory IX final excommunicated Frederick, who responded by leading Crusaders to the Holy Land. _____. Frederick failed to take Egypt, however, and was forced into establishing yet another peace treaty with Sultan al-Kamil.

    A. Unlike many of his predecessors, Frederick's accomplishments in the Sixth Crusade were successes of diplomacy rather than fighting.

    B. The Sixth Crusade resulted in a sectioning off of Jerusalem for both Christian and Muslim rule.

    C. As with previous Crusades, any success was short-lived, and the tides of power shifted once again.

    D. Much to everyone's surprise, Frederick was successful and brought about Christian victories in Jerusalem, Bethlehem, and Nazareth.

23. The Seventh Crusade, which began in 1248, was another feeble attempt against the growing strength of Muslim forces. The Knights Templar who remained in the Holy Land between Crusades found themselves under increasing pressure from powerful Muslim forces, and the Persian Khwarezmian army in particular. By 1248, the Christian Kingdom of Outremer, which was composed of various Christian states throughout the Holy Land, had been virtually destroyed. In response, King Louis IX of France led his warriors to the Near East but with little success. _____.

    A. The Third Crusade, which was prompted by the Muslim successes in Jerusalem in 1187, had created far more interest in Europe.

    B. The Knights Templars, supported by Bedouin mercenaries, were no match for the Khwarezmian warriors.

    C. Louis is said to have spent most of the Seventh Crusade, which lasted until 1254, in the Crusader court at Acre in modern-day Israel.

    D. The failure of the Knights Templar is generally viewed as the reason for the collapse of the Christian states in the Holy Land.

24. The Eighth Crusade, which began in 1270, was King Louis IX's failed second attempt to make a difference in the Holy Land. He called for Crusaders to take up arms once again in order to assist what remained of the Christian kingdom in the Holy Land. As it turned out, Louis's good intentions were greater than his success. The Crusaders were unable to make it to the Holy Land, ending up in Tunis in North Africa instead. There, Louis died only a couple of months after arriving. The king was canonized for his crusading spirit, but the Eighth Crusade is remembered only for Louis's death. _____.

    A. In fact, due to being largely insignificant, the Eighth Crusade is often combined with the Ninth Crusade.
    B. Despite Louis's failure, historians do not blame him, considering that the Ninth Crusade was an equal if not greater failure.
    C. By this time, the remnants of the Christian states were in disarray, and the best efforts of the Crusaders would not have saved them.
    D. King Louis IX remains the only king of France who was canonized for his piety.

25. The Ninth Crusade began as an offshoot of the Eighth Crusade, when Edward Longshanks—later King Edward I of England—picked up where King Louis IX of France had left off. Success was minimal, and the Crusade lasted barely a year, from 1271 to 1272. Following the Ninth Crusade, the Christian warriors attempted to establish a Franco-Mongol alliance with the warrior tribes of the Far East. _____. Defeat became inevitable, as traditionally Christian strongholds at Antioch, Tripoli, and Acre fell to the Muslims. By 1291, the Christians had been soundly defeated and the Near East was firmly in Muslim hands.

    A. The Mongols had been moving in from the east and were gradually encroaching on Muslim holdings in the Holy Land.
    B. While the Mongols experienced some success in defeating the Muslim princedoms, they were unable to effect widespread organization with the Crusaders.
    C. The Mongols were willing to ally themselves with the Christians, and vice versa, in an effort to oppose Muslim strength in the Near East.
    D. The Mamluk warriors of Egypt had sworn to remove Christian holdings from the Near East.

26. Alongside the nine large-scale Crusades to the Holy Land were several smaller Crusades, including the Albigensian Crusade. _____. The Albigenses, also called Cathars, were gnostics who believed that earthly matter was evil, while only spiritual matter was good. As a result, the Catholic Church, which taught that Christ was both fully God and fully man—and thus composed of earthly matter—deemed Albigensian teaching to be heretical. Crusaders from the northern parts of France took up the cross to destroy Cathar heresy and thus place southern France under the control of northern France. The Crusade lasted for several decades, with the last of the Albigensians falling to northern French authority in 1255.

    A. The Albigensian Crusade began in 1209, and many consider it to have been completed in 1229.
    B. This Crusade is named for the heresy it aimed to wipe out from the southern part of France.
    C. Albigensian beliefs were not new but had arisen even in the days of the early Christian Church.
    D. The medieval Catholic Church considered heresy a severe sin and aimed to destroy any heretical beliefs that infected Europe.

27. The event known as the Children's Crusade began in 1212, although modern historians question the accuracy of stories about what occurred. According to tradition, separate groups of children throughout France and Germany joined together to establish a Children's Crusade to the Holy Land. Some accounts place the number of juvenile warriors at upward of 40,000. Having banded together to travel to the Holy Land, they had limited means of reaching their destination, and reports suggest that most, if not all, died during the journey or were sold into slavery. _____.

    A. Medieval travel was difficult even for trained warriors, and those children who were not shipwrecked or starved during their travels would have been easy prey for slave traders along the coasts of North Africa.

    B. Recent examination of the accounts suggest that what the medieval historians referred to as a Children's Crusade was actually a gathering of itinerant people living in poverty who had hoped to change their fortunes in the Holy Land.

    C. The Children's Crusade is believed to have started from the preaching of poor shepherds who called young people to stand up for Christianity and take up the challenge to convert Muslims in the Holy Land to Christianity.

    D. Pope Innocent III is said to have believed in the Children's Crusade and viewed the event as a warning against the failures of adult Christians to take action in the Holy Land.

For Questions 28 and 29, choose the best sentence to follow and develop the topic sentence that is given.

28. Alchemy became popular among medieval scholars when writings of Aristotle and Arabic scientists were discovered.

    A. Plato's works also proved to be important among the alchemists, although they did not rise to the level of importance that Aristotle's did.

    B. The Greeks had recognized that a natural order governs the world, and the Islamic scientists acknowledged the elements that compose all substances.

    C. Among the Islamic scientists, Jabir ibn Hayyan was most famous for his laboratory experiments.

    D. Roger Bacon expanded on the ancient practices through extensive experiments.

29. The alchemists of the Middle Ages worked to convert or "transmute" substances, changing them from one substance into another.

    A. Transmutation was rejected by the Church as a form of stealing from nature and rejecting what God had made.

    B. The ideal source of transmutation was believed to be the coveted "philosopher's stone," which was never found.

    C. The Holy Roman Emperor Rudolf II supported the practice of alchemy.

    D. The most popular transmutation was that of converting basic substances or metals into silver or gold, thus increasing their value.

*For Questions 30 and 31, select the sentence that does **not** belong in the paragraph.*

30. In 1870, the British Parliament passed the Married Women's Property Act. (A) The primary purpose of the act was to provide women with property rights. (B) Prior to the passage of the act, any property a woman owned or wages she made belonged to her husband. (C) Women were also prevented by law from having custody of their children. (D) Once the act went into effect, women could claim the rights to maintain their property and wages in their own names.

    A. A
    B. B
    C. C
    D. D

31. The British Parliament updated the Married Women's Property Act in 1882. (A) Fathers typically provided dowries for their daughters in order to give them some legal income. (B) Traditional laws had held that women had no right to property or wealth and would receive virtually nothing after a divorce. (C) Even women escaping abusive husbands had no right to property that they brought into the marriage if they tried to divorce their husbands. (D) The revised law provided women with further rights in property ownership and in the event of divorce

    A. A
    B. B
    C. C
    D. D

For Questions 32-54, read the sentence and select the correctly written answer to replace each underlined sentence or phrase.

32. Karl and Henry raced to the reservoir, climbed the ladder, and then they dove into the cool water.

    A. raced to the reservoir, climbed the ladder, and then they dove into
    B. first raced to the reservoir, climbed the ladder, and then they dove into
    C. raced to the reservoir, they climbed the ladder, and then they dove into
    D. raced to the reservoir, climbed the ladder, and dove into

33. Did either Tracy or Vanessa realize that her decision would be so momentous?

    A. Tracy or Vanessa realize that her decision would be
    B. Tracy or Vanessa realize that each of their decision was
    C. Tracy or Vanessa realize that her or her decision would be
    D. Tracy or Vanessa realize that their decision would be

34. Despite their lucky escape, Jason and his brother could not hardly enjoy themselves.

    A. Jason and his brother could not hardly enjoy themselves.
    B. Jason and his brother could not enjoy themselves.
    C. Jason and Jason's brother could not hardly enjoy themselves.
    D. Jason and his brother could not enjoy them.

35. Stew recipes call for rosemary, parsley, thyme, and these sort of herbs.

    A. for rosemary, parsley, thyme, and these sort of herbs.
    B. for: rosemary; parsley; thyme; and these sort of herbs.
    C. for rosemary, parsley, thyme, and these sorts of herbs.
    D. for rosemary, parsley, thyme, and this sorts of herbs.

36. Mr. King, an individual of considerable influence, created a personal fortune and gave back to the community.

    A. an individual of considerable influence, created a personal fortune and gave back
    B. an individual of considerable influence, he created a personal fortune and gave back
    C. an individual of considerable influence created a personal fortune and gave back
    D. an individual of considerable influence, created a personal fortune and gave it back

37. She is the person whose opinion matters the most.

    A. She is the person whose opinion matters the most.
    B. She is the person to whom opinion matters the most.
    C. She is the person who matters the most, in my opinion.
    D. She is the person for whom opinion matters the most.

38. Minerals are nutritionally significant elements that assist to make your body work properly.

    A. that assist to make your body
    B. that help your body
    C. that making your body
    D. that work to make your body

39. Of the two, the oldest brother had a much more difficult time in school.

    A. the oldest brother
    B. the older brother
    C. the earliest brother
    D. the best brother

40. The duck waddled towards the pond, her five ducklings following just behind her.

    A. her five ducklings following just behind her
    B. and then there were five ducklings following in back of her
    C. therefore the ducklings were following behind
    D. and so her five ducklings were following just behind her

41. Fair teachers understand that he or she cannot treat any student with favoritism.

    A. Fair teachers understand that he or she
    B. Fair teachers understand that he
    C. Fair teachers understand that she
    D. Fair teachers understand that they

42. We will begin with painting first, and then secondly we will start the decoupage process.

    A. first, and then secondly
    B. firstly, and then secondly
    C. first, and then second
    D. first, then second

43. The hidden passageway in the bowels of the castle remained a well kept secret.

    A. remained a well kept secret
    B. remained a well-kept secret
    C. remained a wellkept secret
    D. was always going to be a secret

44. Another view of the test results had been planned to be provided by a different doctor.

    A. Another view of the test results had been planned to be provided by a different doctor.
    B. She will need to get new test results from a different doctor.
    C. A different doctor has planned to provide another view of the test results.
    D. Several new views of the results are provided and planned with a different doctor.

45. <u>I dare not whisper</u> the deadly secret to a single soul.

    A. I dare not whisper
    B. I should not whisper
    C. I cannot tell anyone
    D. I swore not to tell

46. The scientist said we did need not trouble our minds with trivial details.

    A. The scientist said we did need not trouble
    B. The scientist said we did not trouble
    C. The scientist said do not worry
    D. The scientist said we need not trouble

47. Every teacher ought set a good example for his or her students.

    A. Every teacher ought set a good example
    B. Every teacher ought to set a good example
    C. Teachers are required to set a good example
    D. It is important for teachers to set good examples

48. The Math Committee worked to make sure students <u>had options to participate in</u> contests, book work, computer games or memory practice games.

    A. had options to participate in
    B. met the requirements for
    C. were allowed to do
    D. could choose one of the following:

49. Forgetting to feed the dog was a honest mistake.

    A. Forgetting to feed the dog was a honest mistake.
    B. She honestly forgot to feed the dog.
    C. The dog went hungry.
    D. Forgetting to feed the dog was an honest mistake.

50. On his first day at the news station, the new anchorman had to determine <u>where his desk was at</u>.

    A. where his desk was at
    B. the location of the desk
    C. which desk would belong to him
    D. where his desk was

51. The gentleness of the summer sky while the buttercups shined like the stars.

    A. The gentleness of the summer sky while the buttercups shined like the stars.
    B. There was the gentleness of the summer sky while the buttercups shined like the stars.
    C. The gentle summer sky even as the buttercups shined as though they were stars.
    D. The summer sky gentleness while the buttercups shined like the stars.

52. He got up bright and early and he spent a whole hour taking a shower.

    A. He got up bright and early and he spent
    B. He got up as early as he could and he took
    C. He arose before the dawn; and he spent
    D. He got up bright and early, and he spent

53. The principal added an additional break time into the teachers' busy schedules.

    A. The principal added an additional break time
    B. The principal decided that he needed to add another break time
    C. The principal added another break time
    D. The principal added a third break time

54. The cow cumbersome crossed the wide, grassy field.

    A. The cow cumbersome crossed the wide, grassy field.
    B. The cow cumbersome crossed the wide grassy field.
    C. The cow cumbersomely crossed the wide, grassy field.
    D. The cow did his best to cross the wide, grassy field.

Reading Skills Practice Questions

Read the passage below and answer questions 1-5.

Chang-Rae Lee's debut and award-winning novel <u>Native Speaker</u> is about Henry Park, a Korean-American individual who struggles to find his place as an immigrant in a suburb of New York City. This novel addresses the notion that as the individuals who know us best, our family, peers, and lovers are the individuals who direct our lives and end up defining us. Henry Park is confronted with this reality in the very beginning of the novel, which begins:

The day my wife left she gave me a list of who I was.

Upon separating from his wife, Park struggles with racial and ethnic identity issues due to his loneliness. Through Parks' work as an undercover operative for a private intelligence agency, the author presents the theme of espionage as metaphor for the internal divide that Park experiences as an immigrant. This dual reality creates two worlds for Park and increases his sense of uncertainty with regard to his place in society. While he constantly feels like an outsider looking in, he also feels like he belongs to neither world.

Chang-Rae Lee is also a first-generation Korean American immigrant. He immigrated to America at the early age of three. Themes of identity, race, and cultural alienation pervade his works. His interests in these themes no doubt stem from his first-hand experience as a kid growing up in a Korean household while going to an American school. Lee is also author of <u>A Gesture Life</u> and <u>Aloft</u>. The protagonists are similar in that they deal with labels placed on them based on race, color, and language. Consequently, all of these characters struggle to belong in America.

Lee's novels address differences within a nation's mix of race, religion, and history, and the necessity of assimilation between cultures. In his works and through his characters, Lee shows us both the difficulties and the subtleties of the immigrant experience in America. He urges us to consider the role of borders and to consider why the idea of opening up one's borders is so frightening. In an ever-changing world in which cultures are becoming more intermingled, the meaning of identity must be constantly redefined, especially when the security of belonging to a place is becoming increasingly elusive. As our world grows smaller with increasing technological advances, these themes in Lee's novels become even more pertinent.

1. Which of the following best describes the purpose of this passage?

    A. to criticize

    B. to analyze

    C. to entertain

    D. to inform

2. Why does the author of the passage quote the first line of the novel Native Speaker?

    A. to illustrate one of the themes in the novel

    B. to show how the book is semi-autobiographical

    C. it is the main idea of the novel

    D. to create interest in the novel

3. According to the passage, which of the following is not a main theme of Lee's novels?

    A. identity
    B. culture
    C. immigration
    D. espionage

4. Based on the passage, why do Lee's novels focus on race and cultural identity?

    A. because Lee was born in Korea
    B. because Lee's ancestors are Korean
    C. because Lee immigrated to America at a young age
    D. because Lee feels these issues are the biggest problem facing America

5. How does the author of the passage feel about the ideas presented in Lee's novels?

    A. concerned about the disappearance of cultures in a rapidly expanding and mixed world
    B. excited that immigrants are easily able to redefine and establish themselves in new cultures
    C. certain that all borders will eventually be eliminated so world cultures will commingle and fully assimilate
    D. critical regarding the role technology has played in society and how it destroys the immigrant experience

Read the set of directions below to answer questions 6-9.

> This formula is for people with deficiencies and anemic conditions. It aids in the body's absorption of vital minerals such as iron, calcium, zinc, potassium, and sulfur. Take the following ingredients:
>
> Parsley root Comfrey root
>
> Yellow dock Watercress
>
> Nettles Kelp
>
> Irish moss
>
> Slowly simmer equal parts of these herbs with four ounces to a half-quart of water. Continue to simmer slowly until the volume of liquid is reduced by half. Strain, reserve the liquid, and cover the herbs with water once more. Then simmer again for 10 minutes. Strain and combine the two liquids. Cook the liquid down until the volume is reduced by half. Add an equal amount of blackstrap molasses. Take one tablespoon four to five times daily, not exceeding four tablespoons in a 24-hour period. times daily, not exceeding four tablespoons in a 24-hour period.

6. What is the main reason for taking this formula?

    A. to serve as a mineral supplement
    B. to get rid of unnecessary minerals
    C. to reduce the absorption of minerals
    D. to increase the absorption of minerals

7. If a $\frac{1}{4}$ ounce of yellow dock is used, how much watercress should be used?

    A. $\frac{1}{2}$ ounce

    B. $\frac{1}{4}$ ounce

    C. $\frac{1}{3}$ ounce

    D. 1 ounce

8. If a patient follows the directions correctly, how often could the medicine be taken?

    A. once every two hours
    B. once every four hours
    C. once every three hours
    D. once every six hours

9. Which cooking process is not required to make this formula?

    A. evaporating
    B. filtering
    C. whisking
    D. mixing

Use the data in the table below to answer question 10-14.

Precipitation (inches)			
Date	Albany	Coral Bay	Bunbury
6/1	0.01	0.02	0.02
6/2	0.25	0.35	0.00
6/3	0.55	0.75	0.20
6/4	0.00	0.45	0.10
6/5	0.90	1.01	0.50
6/6	2.00	2.15	1.90
6/7	0.95	1.05	1.15

10. How much more rain did Albany receive than Bunbury on the third of the month?

    A. 0.30 inches
    B. 0.35 inches
    C. 0.55 inches
    D. 0.25 inches

11. What was the average amount of precipitation received in all areas on the fifth of the month?

    A. 0.80 inches
    B. 1.01 inches
    C. 2.41 inches
    D. 0.95 inches

12. On what day was flooding most likely the greatest concern?

   A. first
   B. fifth
   C. sixth
   D. seventh

13. Based on the data in the table, which city has the driest climate?

   A. Albany
   B. Coral Bay
   C. Bunbury
   D. They all have the same climate.

14. Which statement best compares the precipitation between Albany and Coral Bay?

   A. Albany is usually slightly wetter than Coral Bay.
   B. Coral Bay is usually slightly wetter than Albany.
   C. Coral Bay is always much wetter than Albany.
   D. There is no difference between Albany and Coral Bay.

Read the paragraph below to answer questions 15-17.

> The Channel Tunnel is an underwater tunnel that passes through the English Channel and connects England and France. Work on the Tunnel began in 1987 despite much controversy. Many protests took place due to concerns for the environment, fears about terrorism, and the risk of fire. Construction required five thousand workers to dig undersea in the Channel at all hours of the day using laser-guided Tunnel Boring machines. These machines cost around 7.5 million pounds and could construct up to one thousand meters of tunnel a month. Two tunnels were built for passenger trains, with a smaller service tunnel was built in between for maintenance and an escape route in the case of emergency. Costs to construct the Tunnel were much higher than anticipated, and loans were required to finance its construction. After many delays and additional costs, the tunnel was finally opened in 1995. The concrete tunnel's overall length is 50 kilometers, with 40 km being undersea. The journey time from England to France is only 35 minutes, and trains run every 20 minutes. Travel between London and Brussels takes three hours and 10 minutes. In its first year of service, the Tunnel accounted for 40% of the traffic across the Channel and had a turnover of 299 million pounds. Nonetheless, it suffered a huge loss of 925 million pounds due to the high interest the Tunnel company had to pay on the 8.1 billion pounds borrowed from banks.

15. Given that one Tunnel Boring machine could build 1,000 m of tunnel a month and the Tunnel is 50 km long, how fast could the Tunnel have been built using two Tunnel Boring machines if there had been no delays?

   A. just under 5 years
   B. about 1 year
   C. just over 4 years
   D. just over 2 years

- 69 -

16. If a passenger leaves London on the 8:35 a.m. train, what is their expected arrival time in Brussels? (note: Brussels is one time zone east of London)

    A. 9:55 a.m.
    B. 10:10 a.m.
    C. 12:45 p.m.
    D. 1:10 p.m.

17. According to the passage, what was not a reason people were against the construction of the Tunnel?

    A. It will disrupt and pollute marine habitats.
    B. It will take too long to build.
    C. Fires will endanger people and the environment.
    D. It will threaten national security.

Answer questions 18 – 22 based on the debate below.

> *Forest Manager:* Salvage logging is the removal of dead or dying forest stands left behind by a fire or disease. It has been practiced for several decades. Dead or dying trees become fuel that feeds future fires. The best way to minimize the risk of forest fires is to remove the dead timber from the forest floor. Salvage logging followed by replanting ensures the reestablishment of desirable tree species. For instance, planting conifers accelerates the return of fire resistant forests. Harvesting timber benefits forests by reducing fuel load, thinning the forest stands, and relieving competition between trees. Burned landscapes leave behind black surfaces and ash layers that result in very high soil temperatures. These high soil temperatures can kill many plant species. Logging mixes the soil, thereby decreasing surface temperatures to more normal levels. Shade from small, woody material left behind by logging also helps to decrease surface temperatures. After an area has been salvage logged, seedlings in the area begin to regenerate almost immediately; nonetheless, regeneration can take several years in unmanaged areas.

> *Ecology professor:* Salvage logging transfers material like small, broken branches to the forest floor where it is available for fuel. The removal of larger, less flammable trees while leaving behind small dead limbs increases the risk of forest fires. In unmanaged areas, these woody materials are found more commonly on the tops of trees where they are unavailable to fires. Logging destroys old growth forests more resistant to wildfires and creates younger forests more vulnerable to severe fires. In old growth forests, branches of bigger trees are higher above the floor where fires may not reach. Replanting after wildfires creates monoculture plantations in which only a single crop is planted and produced. This monoculture creates less biological diversity and less disease resistant vegetation that in turn increases vulnerability to fire. Salvage logging also interferes with natural forest regeneration by killing most of the seedlings that reemerge on their own after a wildfire. It disrupts the soil, increases erosion, and removes most of the shade needed for young seedlings to grow.

18. According to the professor, how are unmanaged areas advantageous in distributing small, woody materials after a fire?

    A. They are left on the forest floor and provide nutrients to the soil.
    B. They are left on the forest floor and serve as fuel for fires.
    C. They are left on the tops of trees where fires cannot reach.
    D. They are distributed more evenly across the forest floor.

19. A study compared two plots of land that were managed differently after a fire. Plot A was salvage logged, while Plot B was left unmanaged. When a second fire occurred, they compared two plant groups between Plots A and B and found that both plant groups burned with greater severity in Plot A than in Plot B. Which viewpoint do these results support?

    A. only the manager
    B. only the professor
    C. both the manager and professor
    D. neither the manager nor the professor

20. What is the main idea of the forest manager's argument?

    A. Salvage logging is beneficial because it removes dead or dying timber from the forest floor, thereby reducing the risk of future fires.
    B. Salvage logging is beneficial because it has been practiced for several decades.
    C. Salvage logging is harmful because it raises soil temperatures above normal levels and threatens the health of plant species.
    D. Salvage logging is beneficial because it provides shade for seedlings to grow after a wildfire.

21. According to the professor, young forests are more vulnerable to severe fires than old growth forests. Which of the following statements does not support this view?

    A. In younger forests, small branches are closer to the forest floor and more available for fires.
    B. Old growth forests contain larger and taller trees, where branches are high up and fires may not reach.
    C. Younger forests have less biological diversity and less disease-resistant trees.
    D. Larger trees common in old growth forests serve as the main fuel source for severe fires.

22. Whose viewpoints would be validated by a future study looking at the distribution and regeneration of seedlings for several years following a wildfire in both managed and unmanaged forests?

    A. only the manager
    B. only the professor
    C. both the manager and professor
    D. neither the manager nor professor

Use the passage below to answer questions 23-27.

    During the 1800s, Charles Darwin became known for his studies of plants and animals on the Galapagos Islands. He is often referred to as "the father of evolution," because he was first to describe a mechanism by which organisms change over time.

    The Galapagos Islands are situated off the coast of South America. Much of Darwin's work on the islands focused on the birds. He noticed that island birds looked similar to finches on the South American continent and resembled a type of modified finch. The only differences in the finches Darwin saw were in their beaks

- 71 -

and the kind of food they ate. Finches on the mainland were seed-eating birds, but the island finches ate insects, seeds, plant matter, egg yolks, and blood.

Darwin theorized that the island finches were offspring of one type of mainland finch. The population of finches was changing over time due to their environment. He believed the finches' eating habits changed because of the island's limited food supply. As the finches began to eat differently, the way their beaks worked and looked changed as well. For instance, insect-eating finches needed longer beaks for digging in the ground. Seed-eating and nut-eating finches required thicker beaks to crack the seed shells.

The process by which the finches changed happened over many generations. Among the population of beetle-eating finches, those finches born with longer, sharper beaks naturally had access to more beetles than those finches with shorter beaks. As a result, the sharp-beaked, insect-eating finches thrived and produced many offspring, while the short-beaked insect-eating finches gradually died out. The sharp beak was in effect selected by nature to thrive. The same thing happened in each finch population until finches within the same population began to look similar to each other and different from finches of other populations. These observations eventually led Darwin to develop the theory of natural selection.

23. Why is Charles Darwin called "the father of evolution?"

A. because he coined the term "evolution"
B. because he was the first scientist to study species on the Galapagos Islands
C. because he was the first to describe how organisms changed over time
D. because he was the first to suggest that birds adapted to their environment

24. What is the main point of this passage?

A. to inform
B. to entertain
C. to critique
D. to persuade

25. According to the passage, why did finches with sharp, long beaks thrive while other finches died off?

A. They were able to reproduce faster than other types of finches on the island.
B. They were more numerous and eventually outlived the other finches on the island.
C. They were randomly selected by nature to reproduce over other types of finches on the island.
D. They had better access to insects than other types of finches on the island.

26. Based on Darwin's studies on the islands, what could also be inferred about how geography affects the diversity of species?

A. Geographical barriers decrease diversity of a species.
B. Geographical barriers increase diversity of a species.
C. Geographical barriers have an insignificant impact on the diversity of a species.
D. There is no relationship between geographical barriers and the diversity of a species.

- 72 -

27. Which of the following statements correctly compares the finches Darwin observed in the Galapagos Islands with the finches found on the mainland?

    A. The island finches were very similar with no visible differences.
    B. The island finches differed only in the shape of their beaks.
    C. The island finches differed only in size.
    D. The island finches differed in the shape of their beaks and their diet.

Answer questions 28 through 30 based on the paragraph below.

        The Australian town of Bundanoon recently placed a ban on all bottled water to reduce carbon dioxide emissions associated with bottling and transporting the water. Kingston, a local businessman, organized a campaign group called "Bundy on Tap." The group held a vote at the town's Memorial Hall, where 400 people voted in favor of the ban with only two dissenting votes. Free water fountains will be installed across town in an effort to replace bottled water. Ghent, a city in Brussels, has elected Thursdays as "meatless days." Everyone will eat strictly vegetarian meals in an effort to improve overall health and reduce the environmental impact of raising livestock, an industry that accounts for 18 percent of global greenhouse gas emissions. City-financed schools say they will offer only vegetarian meals on the menu on Thursdays.

28. Why do residents of Bundanoon want to ban bottled water?

    A. They want to decrease emissions produced from the bottling and shipping of water.
    B. They want to install water fountains all over town instead of having to buy bottled water.
    C. They want to save on costs associated with bottling and transporting water.
    D. They want to help conserve water due to an increasingly limited supply.

29. Why do residents of Ghent want to restrict the amount of meat consumed by the population?

    A. because the population is obese
    B. because the livestock industry contributes a large amount to greenhouse gases
    C. because they want to support city-financed schools and help them save money
    D. because they are concerned about the treatment of animals

30. Which statement best describes the vote held in Bundanoon over the elimination of bottled water?

    A. The majority is slightly in favor.
    B. They are equally in favor and in opposition.
    C. The majority is in opposition.
    D. The majority is in favor.

Use the information in the table below to answer question 31 – 34.

Information on Hiking Trails in the Area			
Trail	**Length**	**Level of Difficulty**	**Attractions**
1. Beaverton Falls	2.6 miles	Easy	Three waterfalls with picnic areas open May-September; trail is suitable for all ages. End of trail connects to Copper Creek Trail.
2. Silver Bullet	5.5 miles	Easy – Moderate	Follows the Salmon River; fishing allowed July-October. Meets the Toulanne River and connects to the Toulanne Trail.
3. Eagle Eye	8.2 miles	Moderate – Hard	Trail has steep terrain, narrow segments, and switchbacks. Features two waterfalls and excellent panoramic views at the ridge
4. Toulanne	7.5 miles	Moderate	Beautiful rock formations along trail, with close views of canyon walls and Toulanne River. Boat rentals April-November
5. Copper Creek	9.5 miles	Hard	Icy in winter, and many areas require climbing gear. Caving and climbing gear rentals available year-round.

31. Which trail does not connect to another trail?

    A. Beaverton Falls
    B. Silver Bullet
    C. Eagle Eye
    D. Copper Creek

32. This summer the Esperanza family is planning to have their family reunion outdoors surrounded by beautiful scenery. People of all ages are expected to attend. Which trail would be best for them to use?

    A. Beaverton Falls
    B. Eagle Eye
    C. Toulanne
    D. Copper Creek

33. The Cornell family wants to do some fishing in June. Which trail should they choose?

    A. Beaverton Falls
    B. Eagle Eye
    C. Copper Creek
    D. Toulanne

34. If Joey and Katrina hike an average of 3 miles per hour, about how long will it take them if they take the Beaverton Falls trail and follow it through the Copper Creek trail?

    A. 3 hours

    B. $3\frac{1}{2}$ hours

    C. 4 hours

    D. $4\frac{1}{2}$ hours

Read the paragraph below to answer questions 35 – 38.

    Here are the safety rules for novice scuba divers. These rules are essential to ensure a safe and fun experience. Most importantly, listen to your guide's instructions. The maximum depth of any dive is 100 feet. Make a safety stop for a few minutes at about fifteen feet. Always dive with a partner. If you lose your partner or group you may search for them, but only for a minute. If you cannot find them, then resurface. Do not touch or disturb any fauna or flora, as you may get stung or bitten. Also, do not collect anything from the water in order to preserve the health of the ecosystem and not disturb marine life. Only garbage may be removed. In the event that you are caught in a current, stay calm and relax. It is better to float to the surface and signal for help than to fight against the current. Lastly, stay aware of any changing conditions during the dive. Make sure you finish your dive with at least 40 bars of oxygen left in your tank. Consider that if conditions worsen or become unpredictable, it may be necessary to end the dive prematurely.

35. What should a diver do if separated from the group?

    A. Immediately signal for help.
    B. Look for them until they are found.
    C. Look for them for a short period then return to the surface.
    D. Stay in the same place for a long period and wait for them to find you.

36. At what depth should a diver make a safety stop?

    A. 15 feet below the surface
    B. 15 feet above the ocean floor
    C. 85 feet below the surface
    D. a few feet below the surface

37. If the diver sees a school of fish, which of the following would the diver be allowed to do?

    A. touch the fish to assess the texture of its skin
    B. catch the fish to cook for dinner
    C. observe the fish from a distance
    D. poke the fish with a long pole to study its behavior

38. Why might it be important to finish a dive with a minimum of 40 bars of oxygen in the tank?

    A. to avoid running out of oxygen and have extra in case of emergency
    B. to have enough oxygen saved with which to begin the next dive
    C. to have enough oxygen in case you need to swim against a current
    D. it is impossible to know how much oxygen is needed to reach the surface and get back to the boat

Read the paragraph below to answer questions 39 – 44.

EARLY POLITICAL PARTIES

The United States has always been a <u>pluralistic</u> society, meaning it has always embraced many points of view and many groups with different identities. That is not to say that these groups have always seen eye to eye. The first political parties developed in the United States as a result of conflicting visions of the American identity. Many politicians believed that wealthy merchants and lawyers represented the country's true identity, but many others saw <u>it</u> in the farmers and workers who formed the country's economic base.

The event that brought this disagreement to the surface was the creation of the Bank of the United States in 1791. The bank set out to rid the country of the debts it had accumulated during the American Revolution. Until then, each state was responsible for its own debts. The Bank of the United States, however, wanted to assume these debts and pay them off itself. While many people considered this offer to be a good financial deal for the states, many states were uncomfortable with the arrangement because they saw it as a power play by the federal government. If a central bank had control over the finances of individual states, the people who owned the bank would profit from the states in the future. This concern was the basis of the disagreement: Who should have more power, the individual states or the central government?

The Democratic-Republican Party developed to protest the bank, but it came to represent a vision of America with power spread among states. The Federalist Party was established in defense of the bank, but its ultimate vision was of a strong central government that could help steer the United States toward a more <u>competitive</u> position in the world economy.

These different points of view—central government versus separate states—would not be resolved easily. These same disagreements fueled the tension that erupted into the Civil War over half a century later.

39. According to the passage, the word "pluralistic" most nearly means:

    A. Divisive
    B. Conservative
    C. Tolerant
    D. Liberty

40. What is the author's purpose in writing this passage?

    A. To persuade the reader to accept the Federalist Party's point of view.
    B. To explain the disagreements between early American political parties.
    C. To explain the importance of a strong central government.
    D. To criticize the founders of the Bank of the United States.

41. The word "competitive" is used in the passage to mean:

    A. Inferior
    B. Stronger
    C. Partisan
    D. Identity

42. Which of the following best describes the main idea of the passage?

    A. Political parties should emphasize areas of agreement instead of disagreement.

    B. The earliest political parties in the U.S. reflected conflicting interests.

    C. The Federalist Party had a better plan for the America's interests abroad.

    D. The Bank of the United States was not a secure financial institution.

43. In the last sentence of the first paragraph, the pronoun "it" refers to which of the following?

    A. The country's identity.

    B. The future of the country.

    C. State's rights.

    D. A political party.

44. Which of the following statements can be inferred from the second paragraph?

    A. The formation of the Bank of the United States should not have created so much conflict.

    B. Individual states believed that they should not have to share their profits with the central government.

    C. The bank was attempting to swindle the states.

    D. The states were not willing to listen to reason.

Mathematics Computation Practice Questions

1. 4,307 + 1,864
   - A. 5,161
   - B. 5,271
   - C. 6,171
   - D. 6,271

2. 9,645 - 6,132
   - A. 2,513
   - B. 2,517
   - C. 3,412
   - D. 3,513

3. 5,306 - 3,487
   - A. 1,181
   - B. 1,819
   - C. 2,119
   - D. 2,189

4. 893 x 64
   - A. 54,142
   - B. 56,822
   - C. 56,920
   - D. 57,152

5. 707 x 17
   - A. 12,019
   - B. 12,049
   - C. 17,019
   - D. 17,049

6. $7\overline{)917}$
   - A. 131
   - B. 131 R4
   - C. 145
   - D. 145 R4

7. $97\overline{)29294}$
   - A. 302
   - B. 322
   - C. 3002
   - D. 3022

8. 6.8 + 11.3 + 0.06
    A. 17.16
    B. 17.70
    C. 18.16
    D. 18.70

9. 0.28 x 0.17
    A. 0.2260
    B. 0.4760
    C. 0.0226
    D. 0.0476

10. $\frac{0.8}{1.6}$ is equal to
    A. 0.02
    B. 0.05
    C. 0.2
    D. 0.5

11. 0.58 - 0.39=
    A. 0.19
    B. 1.9
    C. 0.29
    D. 2.9

12. $3\frac{1}{8} + 6 + \frac{3}{7} =$
    A. $9\frac{31}{56}$
    B. $9\frac{1}{2}$
    C. $9\frac{21}{56}$
    D. $9\frac{7}{8}$

13. $4\frac{1}{7} - 2\frac{1}{2} =$
    A. $2\frac{5}{14}$
    B. $1\frac{5}{14}$
    C. $1\frac{9}{14}$
    D. $2\frac{9}{14}$

14. $1\frac{1}{4} \times 3\frac{2}{5} \times 1\frac{2}{3} =$
    A. $7\frac{1}{12}$
    B. $5\frac{5}{6}$
    C. $6\frac{7}{12}$
    D. $8\frac{11}{15}$

15. $\frac{3}{5} \div \frac{1}{2}$

    A. $1\frac{1}{5}$

    B. $\frac{3}{10}$

    C. $1\frac{7}{10}$

    D. $\frac{4}{5}$

16. Which of the following is correct?

    A. $\frac{4}{7} = \frac{12}{21}$

    B. $\frac{3}{4} = \frac{12}{20}$

    C. $\frac{5}{8} = \frac{15}{32}$

    D. $\frac{7}{9} = \frac{28}{35}$

17. Find N for the following:

$$\frac{n}{7} = \frac{18}{21}$$

    A. 3
    B. 4
    C. 5
    D. 6

18. Reduce $\frac{14}{98}$ to lowest terms.

    A. $\frac{7}{49}$

    B. $\frac{2}{14}$

    C. $\frac{1}{7}$

    D. $\frac{3}{8}$

19. Express $\frac{68}{7}$ as a mixed fraction.

    A. $9\frac{5}{7}$

    B. $8\frac{4}{7}$

    C. $9\frac{3}{7}$

    D. $8\frac{6}{7}$

20. 40% of 900

    A. 280
    B. 340
    C. 360
    D. 420

21. 3=(?%) of 60

    A. 5

    B. 9

    C. 15

    D. 20

22. 1 is what percent of 25?

    A. 1%

    B. 2%

    C. 3%

    D. 4%

23. Ratio of 4 to 16 = (?)%

    A. 2

    B. 4

    C. 12

    D. 25

24. $\frac{1}{3} = (?)\% \times \frac{5}{6}$

    A. 10

    B. 20

    C. 30

    D. 40

25. 3:15 as a percentage

    A. 5%

    B. 0.05%

    C 2%

    D. 20%

26. 8% as a reduced common fraction

    A. $\frac{4}{50}$

    B. $\frac{4}{5}$

    C. $\frac{2}{5}$

    D. $\frac{2}{25}$

27. $2\frac{1}{2}\%$ of (?) = 6.25

    A. 140

    B. 175

    C. 200

    D. 250

28. 30% as a reduced common fraction

   A. $\frac{30}{100}$

   B. $\frac{1}{30}$

   C. $\frac{23}{10}$

   D. $\frac{3}{10}$

29. 37% as a decimal

   A. 0.0037

   B. 0.037

   C. 0.37

   D. 3.7

30. 12 is 25% of x

   A. 28

   B. 36

   C. 40

   D. 48

31. 32% of x = 96

   A. 208

   B. 250

   C. 280

   D. 300

32. $-4a + 6a + 2a$

   A. $4a$

   B. $-4a$

   C. $8a$

   D. $12a$

33. $(x^2 - 3x + 3) - (x^2 + 3x - 3)$

   A. 0

   B. $2x^2$

   C. $3x - 3$

   D. $-6x + 6$

34. $4y + 5 = 21$

   A. $y = 3$

   B. $y = 4$

   C. $y = 5$

   D. $y = 6$

35. $3(x + 14) = 4(x + 9)$

   A. $x = 4$

   B. $x = 6$

   C. $x = 12$

   D. $x = 15$

36. $4ax^2 - 8ax^2$

    A: $4ax^2$
    B. $-4ax^2$
    C. $12ax^2$
    D. $-12ax^2$

37. $4(x + 2) - 3 + 3(x + 5)$

    A. $x + 23$
    B. $7x + 20$
    C. $4x + 3$
    D. $7x + 9$

38. $4x - 5 = 23$

    A. $x = 4$
    B. $x = 5$
    C. $x = 6$
    D. $x = 7$

39. $2(r + 4) + 8 = (r + 3)4$

    A. $r = -2$
    B. $r = 2$
    C. $r = -4$
    D. $r = 4$

40. 40 is 20% of (?)

    A. 80
    B. 160
    C. 200
    D. 800

Applied Mathematics Practice Questions

1. If 8 people can eat 6 bags of chips, how many people will it take to eat 15 bags of chips?

    A. 16
    B. 18
    C. 20
    D. 22

2. Stefan's scores on his English essays were 75, 65, 80, 95, and 65. What is the average of his test scores?

    A. 65
    B. 66
    C. 71
    D. 76

Use the information below to answer questions 3 through 6.

Gerald does the food shopping for his family of four. He has allocated himself $300 a month to spend. He pays the following amounts each month:

Fresh produce	80
Breads and other grains	35
Frozen foods	45
Meat, seafood and dairy	90
Other	50

3. Which percentage below is closest to the percentage of Gerald's budget for the "other" category to his entire food budget?

    A. 0.016
    B. 0.16
    C. 1.66
    D. 16.66

4. How much does Gerald spend annually on his food shopping?

    A. $3000
    B. $3300
    C. $3600
    D. $3900

5. Which of the following statements is true?

    A. The money Gerald spends on produce, breads and grains, and frozen foods is more than half his entire food budget
    B. The money Gerald spends on produce, breads and grains, and frozen foods is less than half his entire food budget
    C. The money Gerald spends on produce, breads and grains, and frozen foods is equal to half his entire food budget
    D. The money Gerald spends on produce, breads and grains, and frozen foods is equal to his entire food budget

6. If Gerald spends $10 of his "other" budget on canned beans, what percentage of his "other" budget does his spending on canned beans represent?

    A. 10
    B. 20
    C. 25
    D. 30

7. Ma'Tia drove 400 miles in 6 hours. She has an additional 180 miles to drive. If she drives at the same rate of speed, how long will it take her rounded to the nearest hour?

    A. 1 hour
    B. 2 hours
    C. 3 hours
    D. 4 hours

8. What is the solution for the equation $x/3 + 4 = 7$

    A. 21
    B. 15
    C. 12
    D. 9

9. A pizza dough recipe calls for 2 cups of flour and $1\frac{1}{2}$ teaspoons of salt. How much salt would you need if you wanted to triple the recipe?

    A. 1 tablespoon
    B. 3 teaspoons
    C. $4\frac{1}{2}$ teaspoons
    D. 6 teaspoons

10. If Sherry won a sweepstakes that gave her $1000 a day for every non-weekend day, approximately how much money would she be given in one year?

    A. $365,000
    B. $260,000
    C. $52,000
    D. $24,000

11. The five events hosted last year by the event company, "We Plan It," drew crowds of 175, 320, 417, 533, and 210 people. What is their average attendance for those events?

    A. 231
    B. 271
    C. 331
    D. 371

12. If my local grocery store last year had a total income of $7,056,238 and expenses of $3,998,100, how much profit did it make (profit is income minus expenses)?

    A. $3,058,138
    B. $3,158,138
    C. $2,738,188
    D. $4,158,188

13. Which of the following is true?

A. -(-(-4)) is greater than -3
B. -(-(-7)) is greater than -17 plus 10
C. -4 is greater than the absolute value of -4
D. -10 is greater than -(-(-15))

14. What do you get if you subtract -4 – (-9)?

A. 5
B. -5
C. -13
D. 13

15. 184,770 is the product of 12,318 and what other number

A. 13
B. 14
C. 15
D. 16

16. Tyler is one year older than 3 times Clay's age. The sum of their ages is 21. How old is Tyler?

A. 6
B. 16
C. 5
D. 15

17. What is 0.09356 – 0.003784?

A. 0.00089776
B. 0.0089776
C. 0.089776
D. 0.89776

18. If the 8 people in the room wearing jeans constitute 40% of the people in the room, how many people are there total in the room?

A. 60
B. 40
C. 20
D. 10

19. Jerome wants to enlarge his favorite painting by 20% (length and width). If it is currently 20 inches by 30 inches, what will the area of the enlarged painting be?

A. 600 inches
B. 864 inches
C. 726 inches
D. 926 inches

20. What is the product of (-4)(-2)(-6)?

A. -24
B. 24
C. -48
D. 48

21. How many cubic inches are in a box 10" wide, 3" deep and 14" long?

    A. 420

    B. 4200

    C. 210

    D. 2100

Use the following information to answer questions 22-24.

Grade Distribution Final Examination	
Number of Students	Grade
10	A
14	B
8	C
6	D
2	F

22. What percentage of the total number of students got a B on the final examination?

    A. 20

    B. 25

    C. 30

    D. 35

23. How many more students got either a C or a B than got either a D or an F?

    A. 8

    B. 10

    C. 12

    D. 14

24. What is the ratio of the students who got an F to the students who got an A?

    A. $\frac{1}{20}$

    B. $\frac{1}{10}$

    C. $\frac{1}{5}$

    D. $\frac{2}{5}$

25. What is the perimeter of a park that is 300 yards long and 640 yards wide?

    A. 1880

    B. 192,000

    C. 940

    D. 19,200

26. Solve the equation: $2^3 + (4 + 1)$.

    A. 9

    B. 13

    C. 15

    D. 21

27. Restaurant customers tip their server only 8 percent for poor service. If their tip was $3.70, how much was their bill?

    A. $40.15
    B. $44.60
    C. $46.25
    D. $50.45

28. Enrique weighs 5 pounds more than twice Brendan's weight. If their total weight is 225 pounds, how much does Enrique weigh?

    A. 125 pounds
    B. 152 pounds
    C. 115 pounds
    D. 165 pounds

29. A pasta salad was chilled in the refrigerator at 35° F overnight for 9 hours. The temperature of the pasta dish dropped from 86° F to 38° F. What was the average rate of cooling per hour?

    A. 4.8°/hr
    B. 5.3°/hr
    C. 5.15°/hr
    D. 0.532°/hr

30. Loral received all her grades for the semester (in parentheses) along with the weight for each grade, shown below. What is her final grade?

Weight

        45% = 3 tests (80%, 75%, 92%)
        25% = final (88%)
        15% = paper (91%)
        15% = 2 oral quizzes each worth 25 points (22, 19)

    A. 88
    B. 86
    C. 79
    D. 85

31. The following items were purchased at the grocery store. What was the average price paid for the items?

Item	Cost	Quantity
Milk	$3.50/carton	2
Banana	$0.30 each	5
Can of soup	$1.25/can	3
Carrots	$0.45/stick	6

    A. $0.34
    B. $0.55
    C. $0.93
    D. $1.38

32. Find $(27 \div 9) \times (\sqrt{25} \times 2)$.
    A. 90
    B. 12
    C. 45
    D. 30

33. What is the missing number in the sequence: 4, 6, 10, 18, __, 66.
    A. 22
    B. 34
    C. 45
    D. 54

34. Rick renovated his home. He made his bedroom 40% larger (length and width) than its original size. If the original dimensions were 144 inches by 168 inches, how big is his room now if measured in feet?
    A. 12 ft x 14 ft
    B. 16.8 ft x 19.6 ft
    C. 4.8 ft x 5.6 ft
    D. 201.6 ft x 235.2 ft

35. There are 64 fluid ounces in a ½ gallon. If Nora fills a tank that holds 8 ¾ gallons, how many ounces will she use?
    A. 560 ounces
    B. 1,024 ounces
    C. 1,088 ounces
    D. 1,120 ounces

36. Shaylee goes shopping for two types of fruit: mangoes that cost $2.00 each and coconuts that cost $4.00 each. If she buys 10 pieces of fruit and spends $30.00, how many pieces of each type of fruit did she buy?
    A. 4 mangoes and 6 coconuts
    B. 5 mangoes and 5 coconuts
    C. 6 mangoes and 4 coconuts
    D. 7 mangoes and 3 coconuts

Use the graph below to answer questions 37 and 38.

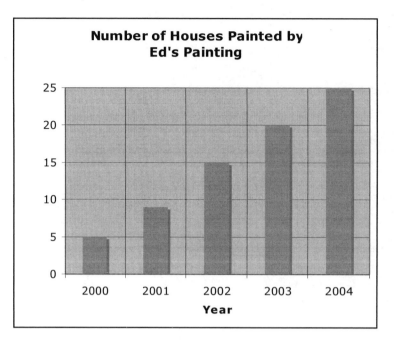

37. What is the average number of houses Ed painted each year from 2000 to 2004?

    A. 15
    B. 74
    C. 12
    D. 22

38. Assuming Ed's Painting did not experience any major business changes, which of the following is likely to be closest to the number of houses he painted in 2005?

    A. 25
    B. 31
    C. 22
    D. 45

39. Which of the following values is *not* equal to 12(45 – 8)?

    A. 540 – 96
    B. 12 x 45 – 12 x 8
    C. (-8 + 45) 12
    D. 45 (12 – 8)

40. A house is 25 feet tall and a ladder is set up 35 feet away from the side of the house. Approximately how long is the ladder from the ground to the roof of the house?

    A. 43 ft
    B. 25 ft
    C. 50 ft
    D. 62 ft

Use the following table to answer questions 41 – 43.

Mrs. McConnell's Classroom	
Eye Color	**Number of Students**
Brown	14
Blue	9
Hazel	5
Green	2

41. What percentage of students in Mrs. McConnell's classroom have either hazel or green eyes?

    A. 23%

    B. 30%

    C. 47%

    D. 77%

42. How many more students have either brown or blue eyes than students who have hazel or green eyes?

    A. 23

    B. 7

    C. 16

    D. 14

43. What is the ratio of students with brown eyes to students with green eyes?

    A. 1:2

    B. 3:1

    C. 1:5

    D. 7:1

44. On a map, the space of $\frac{1}{2}$ of an inch represents 15 miles. If two cities are $4\frac{3}{5}$ inches apart on the map, what is the actual distance between the two cities?

    A. 138 miles

    B. 39 miles

    C. 23 miles

    D. 125 miles

45. A soda company is testing a new sized can to put on the market. The new can is 6 inches in diameter and 12 inches in height. What is the volume of the can in cubic inches?

    A. 339

    B. 113

    C. 432

    D. 226

46. A garden has a perimeter of 600 yards. If the length of the garden is 250 yards, what is the garden's width?

    A. 25

    B. 50

    C. 175

    D. 350

47. Which of the following values is greatest?

A. -4 minus 10
B. -25 – (-30)
C. 4(-20)
D. -2(-10)

48. A farmer set up a rain gauge in his field and recorded the following daily precipitation amounts over the course of a week: 0.45 inches, 0.0 inches, 0.75 inches, 1.20 inches, 1.1 inches, 0.2 inches, and 0.0 inches. What was the average precipitation over that week?

A. 0.74 in
B. 1.05 in
C. 0.53 in
D. 3.70 in

49. Tony has the following number of T-shirts in his closet:

    White - 5
    Black - 2
    Blue - 1
    Yellow - 3

If Tony's electricity goes out, how many T-shirts would he have to pull out of his closet to make sure he has a yellow T-shirt?

A. 4
B. 8
C. 9
D. 11

50. Enrique is a full-time employee who earns $12.00 per hour. If he works overtime, he receives time-and-a-half (where each hour worked over 40 hours is compensated at 1.5 times the regular rate). If Enrique works 45 hours, how much money will he earn?

A. $540
B. $570
C. $510
D. $600

Answer Key Explanations

Language Answers

1. C: The phrase "the tulip breaking virus" needs commas on each side of it to improve clarity in the flow of thought by creating a natural pause in the sentence where this expression occurs.

2. A: A comma is necessary between the words "stocks" and "futures" to indicate the presentation of items in a series or list. (An extra comma could be placed before the conjunction, but it is not essential in this case.)

3. B: This sentence is actually two sentences that need to be separated after the date. The statement "there were no bids" begins a new sentence and thus requires an indication of a break in the thought. (A semicolon or even a colon would also be acceptable to separate the two sentences.)

4. D: The phrase *have to* makes the sentence grammatically correct. The speaker is trying to express that his group was forced to try hard. For this reason, it is essential for the verb *have* to be used. *Have* is an auxiliary verb indicating obligation. It agrees with the first-person plural pronoun *we*. An auxiliary verb accompanies another verb and makes some alterations in mood or tense. In this case, the addition of the verb have indicates that the speaker and others were obliged to try hard. *Can*, *will*, and *have* are all common examples of auxiliary verbs.

5. D: The word *which* makes the sentence grammatically correct. In this sentence, *which* is used as a relative pronoun. A relative pronoun introduces a relative clause, which is so called because it "relates" to the antecedent. The antecedent is the word that the relative pronoun refers to. In this sentence, the antecedent is "French braid," and the subsequent relative clause gives the reader more information about the French braid. Answer choice C is also a relative pronoun, but it is rarely used after a comma.

6. D: The word *began* properly completes the sentence. The sentence begins with the phrase "the other day," which indicates that the action described took place sometime in the recent past. A past tense verb form is appropriate, then. The verb *begun* is the past participle of *begin*. A past participle describes action that took place before but is now complete. This sentence does not indicate, however, that the action is now complete. For all we know, Stan could still be reviewing his class notes. For this reason, the past tense *began* is the correct answer.

7. A: The earliest recording of a human voice was made by Thomas Edison in 1877, when they recorded himself reciting "Mary Had a Little Lamb."

     Error: Pronoun-antecedent agreement

Thomas Edison is singular, so the plural pronoun "they" is incorrect. It should read "he."

8. B: Our basement floods once a yearly.

     Error: Adjective/adverb

Here the adverb "yearly" is incorrectly used. It should be replaced with the noun "year."

9. D: No error.

10. B: The spread of Islam began around 600 A.D. and reached from the Middle East to North Africa, Spain, Central Asia, and India?

Error: Punctuation

Since this is a declarative sentence and not a question, the question mark should be a period.

11. C: The names of the days of the week originate in either Latin or Saxon names for deities, Sunday, for instance, is Saxon for "Sun's Day," while Thursday derives from "Thor's Day."

Error: Comma Splice

There are two complete sentences here joined by only a comma. A period or semicolon should replace the comma after "deities."

12. D: No error.

13. A: Ironically, the namesake of the Nobel Peace Prize, Alfred Nobel, are most noted for his invention of dynamite in the 1860s.

Error: Subject-verb disagreement

The subject of this sentence is the singular noun "namesake." The plural verb "are" is incorrect. It should be replaced with the singular verb "is."

14. A: Loud sounds can causing damage to the hair cells that turn sound waves into electrical signals, which the brain perceives as sound.

Error: Verb tense

The verb "causing" is the progressive tense, which is the incorrect tense for this sentence. The sentence should read, "Loud sounds can cause...."

15. C: Carbon monoxide Poisoning can cause disorientation and delirium, and it can induce a coma.

Error: Capitalization

The word "poisoning" does not need to be capitalized because it is not a proper noun.

16. D: No error.

17. A: They closed the parking deck at midnight, so we could not get no cars out until morning.

Error: Double negative

The phrase "could not get no" is an example of a double negative. The phrase should read, "could not get any ...."

18. A: This answer choice provides the hint of contrast that is necessary between the two clauses. Answer choice B is accurate but fails to offer the sense of contradiction that is needed. Answer choice C makes little sense and cannot be correct. Answer choice D is ineffective with the semicolon, because this form of punctuation limits the flow of thought within the sentence.

19. C: This is one of the rare cases where a colon is the best way to join the two sentences. A colon indicates that the material on the second side of the clause defines the material on the first side of the clause. The second side of the clause indicates the novels that Sir Walter Scott wrote and contributed to his fame as a novelist. Answer choice A makes the sentence read awkwardly. Answer choice B creates a sense of contradiction that is inappropriate to the context of the sentences. Answer choice D also indicates a contrast and cannot be correct.

20. B: This option provides an appositive phrase that combines the sentences with the best flow of thought. Answer choices A and D make no sense because of the indication of contrast that does not exist in the context of the original sentences. Answer choice C makes the sentences more confusing and cannot be correct.

21. A: This answer choice provides the indication of contradiction that is appropriate in the context of the two sentences. Answer choice B is not inaccurate, but it is also not the *best* combination of the sentences. Answer choice C does not make much sense by creating chronology, and answer choice D makes poor use of the colon, because the second clause does not define the first clause.

22. D: Answer choice D moves the paragraph along most effectively by explaining that Frederick brought about victories "in Jerusalem, Bethlehem, and Nazareth." What is more, answer choice D offers the information that is necessary to explain the contrast in the use of "however" within the sentence that follows. Answer choice A has no clear place in the paragraph, and answer choice B is largely irrelevant to the information that is contained within the paragraph. Answer choice C functions more as a final sentence but does not clearly follow the sentence that precedes it or introduce the sentence that follows.

23. C: Answer choice C clarifies the second-to-last sentence in the paragraph by explaining the "little success" of Louis's Crusade. Answer choice A is incorrect, because it focuses more on the Third Crusade than on the Seventh, which is the topic of the paragraph. Answer choice B is insufficient, because it returns the focus to the Knights Templar, which is not the main point but rather a supporting element of the main point. In the same way, answer choice D creates an irrelevant ending by focusing on the Knights Templar rather than the Crusade as a whole.

24. A: Answer choice A offers clear information about the problems of the Eighth Crusade and its results by using the expression "In fact" to follow the mention of the Crusade being "remembered only for Louis's death." Answer choice B has little relevance to the paragraph, and answer choice C is more of an opinion than a clear conclusion for the paragraph. Answer choice D adds what may be described as a tidbit of information, but it does not clearly function as the end of the paragraph and cannot be correct.

25. B: This sentence provides the necessary link about what occurs with the Mongols and why they were unsuccessful, which is indicated in the sentence that follows. Answer choice A expands too much on the Mongol history, which is not appropriate to the topic of the paragraph. Answer choice C seems to delay the progress of the paragraph with unnecessary focus on the motive behind the Franco-Mongol alliance. Answer choice D provides an unnecessary focus on the Mamluk warriors.

26. B: Answer choice B offers a focused definition of the Crusade and how it received its name, thus creating a clear progress of thought between the topic sentence and the sentences that follow. Answer choice A could work, except that the final sentence in the paragraph claims the last Albigensian stronghold fell in 1255, thus negating the date expressed in answer choice A. Answer choice C focuses unnecessarily on the relationship between Albigensian beliefs and those dating from the days of the early Christian Church. Answer choice D stalls the paragraph excessively by

explaining the position of the medieval Church regarding heresy. Answer choice B does this more effectively and is thus correct.

27. B: Answer choice B creates a useful link to the topic sentence by expanding on it more fully, after explaining the traditional views about the Children's Crusade. Answer choice A is interesting but dwells too much on why the children were unsuccessful—when the focus of the paragraph is more on the story about the Crusade and the historical problems about it that have arisen. Answer choice C is an ineffective conclusion to the paragraph and leaves it in need of further information. In the same way, answer choice D is interesting but does not end the paragraph as effectively as answer choice B.

28. B: Answer choice B provides the details of the types of writings that were uncovered and why they might have been of interest to alchemists. Answer choices A, C, and D are interesting and might have a place somewhere in the sentence, but the flow of thought does not point naturally to these statements without further explanation.

29. D: This statement explains *why* alchemists were so focused on converting one substance into another. Answer choices A and C, again, are interesting and might have a place later in the paragraph, but they do not follow as naturally as answer choice D. Answer choice B is vaguely related to the idea of transmutation, but it occurs more as a side note than a useful follow-up statement to the topic sentence.

30. C: The paragraph discusses the purpose behind and the effects of the Married Women's Property Act of 1870. The statement regarding a woman's right (or lack thereof) to have custody of her children is out of place within the context of the paragraph.

31. B: While a statement about dowries that would give a daughter income during her marriage is interesting, it does not fit the rest of the paragraph, which discusses the revised Married Women's Property Act of 1882.

32. D: The verb structure should be consistent in a sentence with parallel structures.

33. A: The singular pronoun *her* is appropriate since the antecedents are joined by *or.* Also, the subjunctive verb form is required to indicate something indefinite.

34. B: The combination of *hardly* and *not* constitutes a double negative.

35. C: The plural demonstrative adjective *these* should be used with the plural noun *sorts.*

36. A: This sentence contains a number of parallel structures that must be treated consistently.

37. A: In this sentence, *whose* is the appropriate possessive pronoun to modify *opinion.*

38. B: Answer choice B is precise and clear. Answer choice A keeps the meaning, but is awkward and wordy. Answer choice C uses the wrong verb tense. Answer choice D would put the word *work* into the sentence twice. It is not completely incorrect, but it is not the best choice.

39. B: When comparing two people or things, the correct comparative word would be *older* rather than *oldest.* If there were more than two, you would use the comparative word *oldest.* The other choices change the intended original meaning of the sentence. The same is true for the comparative words *better* and *best* or *less* and *least.*

40. A: The sentence is precise and clear in its original form. This type of sentence is an absolute construction, including a noun and a modifier. Absolute constructions squeeze two sentences into one. In this case the modifier is a participle phrase.

41. D: The plural subject *teachers* agrees with the pronoun *they*. Pronouns have to agree with gender, number and person. If the subject had been singular, such as *teacher*, then the pronoun would have needed to also be singular. In that case the correct sentence might have been: A fair teacher understands that he or she cannot treat any student with favoritism.

42. C: When putting things or people in order, the words must agree in the series. You can use *first, second, third,* and so forth, or you may use *firstly, secondly, thirdly,* and so forth. In this sentence, answer choice C is the best choice because the two words *first* and *second* agree in the series, and in this case it sounds better. *Firstly* and *secondly* sound awkward. Also, it is correct to use *and then* in the sentence rather than answer choice D which uses only the word *then*.

43. B: *Well* and *kept* put together forms a compound adjective. In this case the compound adjective was written with an adverb and a past participle. When the two together come before and modify a noun, such as *secret*, they must be hyphenated as such: *well-kept secret.*

44. C: The style in the original sentence is awkward because it has a double passive voice. Change the first passive verbs into an active verb and the sentence will simply sound better. Even though answer choice B sounds good and is grammatically correct, you cannot choose it because of the pronoun *she*. The original sentence does not specify gender.

45. A: The sentence is clear and precise in its original form.

46. D: The word *need* is being used as an auxiliary verb in this sentence. It does not go together with *did* or any form of *do* unless it is being used as a main verb. The following is an example of *need* being used as a main verb together with *do: We do need to trouble our minds.*

47. B: The word *ought* is an auxiliary verb that should go together with the word *to* in formal writing. It is sometimes used in speech without the word *to* (especially in particular regions), but is not considered correct in written English. There are some cases where *ought* can be correctly used without *to* in questions, such as: *Ought the teacher set a good example?*

48. A: The sentence is clear and precise in its original form.

49. D: The only problem with the sentence is the use of the adjective *a* rather than *an*. You cannot assume gender (such as *she* or *her*).

50. D: The use of the word *at* at the end of the sentence is unnecessary. It is a dangling preposition. Remove the word *at* to make it clear and precise.

51. B: The original sentence has dependent clauses with words that LOOK like verbs but do not ACT like verbs. The entire sentence is a fragment. Answer choice B is the only one that adds a subject and verb to change the fragment into a complete sentence.

52. D: The original is a run-on sentence. There should be a comma to separate the two thoughts. The use of a semicolon only works if you remove the word *and*, as follows: He got up bright and early; he spent a whole hour taking a shower.

53. C: The two words *added* and *additional* are redundant. Grammatically, it is not wrong, but the two words are similar enough that they seem like the same word. It is awkward. Taking out the *additional* makes the sentence more precise without changing any of the meaning.

54. C: The word *cumbersome* is an adjective, but the placement in the sentence calls for an adverb. Add *ly* to the word to make modify the verb. If it had been used as an adjective, it would have come before the noun as follows: *the cumbersome cow*.

Reading Skill Answers

1. B: The passage was written to analyze the works by Chang-Rae Lee and the themes presented in his most famous novels.

2. A: The author of this passage uses the first line of the novel to provide an example of one of the themes of the novel.

3. D: Espionage is part of the plot of the novel <u>Native Speaker</u>, but it is not a theme that recurs in Lee's works.

4. C: The passage states that Lee's interests in cultural identity and race emerge from his own experiences with these issues as a young immigrant to America.

5. A: The tone of the last paragraph suggests concern over the preservation of cultural identities in an increasingly mixed and expanding world.

6. D: The passage indicates that the formula increases or boosts the absorption of minerals in the body.

7. B: The directions say to mix equal parts of all the herbs listed.

8. D: The dosage indicates not to exceed four tablespoons in a 24-hour period, so the patient should take it no more than every six hours.

9. C: All methods are used in the cooking process except for whisking.

10. B: Albany received 0.55 inches of rain, while Bunbury received only 0.20 in. 0.55 – 0.20 = 0.35 inches.

11. A: Looking at the fifth day of the month, you get: 0.90 + 1.01 + 0.50 = 2.41 ÷ 3 = 0.80.

12. C: Flooding would be of greatest concern on the day that received the most rain in each location, the 6th.

13. C: By summing the total amount of precipitation received over the week, Bunbury received less than Albany and Coral Bay.

14. B: By comparing the differences between Albany and Coral Bay, Coral Bay is typically a little wetter on average than Albany.

15. D: In one month, 2,000 m or 2 km of tunnel could be built with 2 machines. 2 km/1 month = 50 km/x; 2x = 50; x = 25 months, or just over 2 years.

16. C: It takes 3 hrs and 10 mins to travel from London to Brussels, so with the one hour time change, a person on the 8:35 a.m. train would arrive in Brussels at 12:45 p.m., local time.

17. B: The passage does not say anything about concerns over how long the construction would take to complete.

18. C: The professor argues that after a fire, small, woody material is left on the tops of trees where a fire cannot reach. Therefore, the material is unavailable as fuel for future fires.

19. B: Since the plot that was salvage logged (Plot A) burned with greater severity than the unmanaged plot (Plot B), the study supports the professor's view that salvage logging increases the risk and severity of fire.

20. A: The forest manager feels that by removing dead or dying material through salvage logging, less fuel is available for future fires.

21. D: The professor states the opposite of answer choice D and says that larger trees found in old growth forests are more resistant to fire than small, younger trees.

22. C: A study looking at the regeneration of seedlings in both logged and unmanaged forests would help to clarify and/or validate both arguments, since both the manager and the professor discuss the importance of seedling growth following a fire.

23. C: The passage states that he was given this title since he was the first to explain how organisms change over time.

24. A: The tone and purpose of this passage is to inform the reader.

25. D: The passage explains that finches with longer, sharper beaks were able to reach insects more easily than finches with shorter beaks, giving them an advantage over the other finches on the island.

26. B: The island finches were different from the mainland finches, so their geographical separation over time increased the diversity of finches.

27. D: The passage states that the island finches differed from the mainland finches by the shape of their beaks and in their diet.

28. A: While the other answer choices may be valid reasons, the passage clearly states that residents hope to reduce emissions associated with bottling and transporting the water.

29. B: The passage states that residents want to lessen the impact raising livestock has on the environment, namely to reduce the emissions from the livestock industry.

30. D: There is a majority in favor of the ban, with 400 people for it and only 2 people against it.

31. C: The Eagle Eye Trail is the only trail that does not connect to one of the other trails.

32. A: The Beaverton Falls trail is an easy trail and says that it is suitable for people of all ages. It also offers picnic areas. The other trails listed are moderate to hard and do not offer areas to picnic.

33. D: According to the table, the Toulanne Trail offers boat rentals as early as May; whereas, the Silver Bullet Trail does not allow fishing until July.

34. C: The total distance they will hike is 2.6 miles + 9.5 miles =12.1 miles. If they hike 3 miles per hour, it will take them 12.1/3 = 4.03 hours to hike 12.1 miles.

35. C: According to the passage, a diver should spend only a moment looking for others in the group. If the others cannot be found, the diver should resurface.

36. A: The passage states that a safety stop should be made fifteen feet down, or below the surface.

37. C: Since a diver is not allowed to touch or disturb the fauna in any way, the only activity the diver is allowed to do is observe the fish.

38. A: The passage implies that the diver should have enough oxygen left in the tank in case something goes wrong, he or she gets lost, or some other unforeseen complication arises.

39. C: The passage states that a pluralistic society means one that embraces "many points of view," which is closest in meaning to choice C, "tolerant."

40. B: This passage does not choose one point of view on the issue, so only choice B is in keeping with the passage's purpose, which is to explain the disagreements between the earliest political parties in the US.

41. B: The word competitive means that the country would be able to compete financially with other countries. Choice B, stronger, is the best choice.

42. B: The passage explains the conflicting interests these two political parties represent. Choice B best reflects that point.

43. A: It refers to the noun "identity." Choice A is the best choice.

44. B: Since the passage does not choose to argue a particular point of view, the best choice would be the most neutral statement, choice B.

Mathematics Computation Answers

1. D: This is a simple addition problem with carrying. Start with the ones column and add 7+4, write down the 1 and add the 1 to the digits in the tens column. Now add 0+6+1. Write down the 7. Now add 3+8 and write down the 1. Add the 1 to the thousands column. Add 4+1+1 and write the 6 to get the answer 6271.

2. D: This is a simple subtraction problem. Start with the ones column and subtract 5-2, then 4-3, then 6-1, then 9-6 to get 3,513.

3. B: This is a subtraction problem which also involves borrowing. Start with the ones column. Since 7 can't be subtracted from 6, borrow ten from the tens column. Cross out the 0 and make it a 9. Cross out the 3 in the hundreds column and make it a 2. Now subtract 7 from 16. Write down 9. Move to the tens column. Subtract 8 from 9 and write down 1. Move to the hundreds column. Since you can't subtract 4 from 3, borrow ten from the thousands column. Cross out the 5 and make it a 4. 12-4= 8. Now subtract 3 from 4 and write down 1 to get 1819.

4. D: This is a multiplication problem with carrying. Start with the ones column. Multiply 4 by each digit in above it beginning with the ones column. Write down each product: going across it will read 3572. Now multiply 6 by each of the digits above it. Write down each product: going across it will read 5358. Ensure that the 8 is in the tens column and the other numbers fall evenly to the right. Now add the numbers like a regular addition problem to get 57,152

5. A: This is a multiplication problem with 0. Start with the 7 in 17 and multiply it by each of the digits at the top 7 x 7. Write down the 9 and place the 4 in the tens column. 7 x 0 is 0. Add the 4. 7 x 7 is 49. The top line will read 4949. Now multiply 1 by 7. Write down the 7. 1 x 0 is 0 and 1 x 7 is 7. The bottom line will read 707.Add these together with the 7 in the tens column and the answer will be 12,019.

6. A: This is a simple division problem. Divide the 7 into 9. It goes in 1 time. Write 1 above the 9 and subtract 7 from 9 to get 2. Bring down the 1 and place it beside the 2. Divide 7 into 21. It goes in 3 times. Divide 7 into 7. It goes 1 time. .

7. A: This is a simple division problem. Divide 97 into 292. It goes in 3 times. Write 3 above the second 2 and subtract 291 from 292. The result is 1. Bring down the 9. Since 19 cannot be divided into 97, write a zero next to the 3. Bring down the 4. Divide 97 into 194. It goes 2 times.

8. C: This is a simple addition problem. Line up the decimals so that they are all in the same place in the equation, and see that there is a 6 by itself in the hundredths column. Then add the tenths column: 8+3to get 11. Write down the 1 and carry the 1. Add the ones column: 6+1 plus the carried 1. Write down 8. Then write down the 1.

9. D: This is multiplication with decimals. Multiply the 7 by 8 to get 56. Put down the 6 and carry the 5. Multiply 7 by 2 to get 14. Add the 5. Write 19 to left of 6. Multiply the 1 by the 8 to get 8. Multiply 1 by 2 to get 2. Add the two lines together, making sure that the 8 in the bottom figure is even with the 9. Get 476. Count 4 decimal points over (2 from the top multiplier and 2 from the second multiplier) and add a 0 before adding the decimal.

10. D: To solve, divide 1.6 into .8. Move the decimal in 16 over 1 place to make it 16. Because this decimal point was moved 1 places, it must be done to the other decimal too. .8 becomes 8. Now divide 16 into 8 (not 8 into 16).

11. A: This is a simple subtraction problem with decimals. Line up the decimals and subtract 9 from 8. Since this can't be done, borrow 10 from the 5. Cross out the 5 and make it 4. Now subtract 9 from 18 to get 9. Subtract 3 from 4 and get 1. Place the decimal point before the 1.

12. A: To add fractions, ensure that the denominator (the number on the bottom) is the same. Since it is not, change them both to 56ths. 1/8 equals 7/56. 3/7 equals 24/56. Now add the whole numbers: 3+6 = 9 and the fractions 31/56.

13. C: To subtract fractions, ensure that the denominator (the number on the bottom) is the same. Since it is not, change them both to 14ths. 1/7 = 2/14; 1/2 = 7/14. The equation now looks like this: $4\frac{2}{14} - 2\frac{7}{14}$. Change the 4 to 3 and add 14 to the numerator (the top number) so that the fractions can be subtracted. The equation now looks like this: $3\frac{16}{14} - 2\frac{7}{14}$. Subtract: $1\frac{9}{14}$

14. A: To multiply mixed numbers, first create improper fractions. Multiply the whole number by the denominator, then add the numerator. $1\frac{1}{4}$ becomes $\frac{5}{4}$; $3\frac{2}{5}$ becomes $\frac{17}{5}$; $1\frac{2}{3}$ becomes $\frac{5}{3}$.

The problem will look like this: $\frac{5}{4} \times \frac{17}{5} \times \frac{5}{3} = \frac{425}{60} = 7\frac{5}{60} = 7\frac{1}{12}$.

15. A: To divide fractions, change the second fraction to its reciprocal (its reverse) and multiply: $\frac{3}{5} \times \frac{2}{1}$

16. A: To solve, test each answer. Notice the in (A), the numerator has been multiplied by 3 to get 12. The denominator has been multiplied by 3 to get 21. In (B) the numerator has been multiplied by 4 and the denominator has been multiplied by 5. In (C), the numerator has been multiplied by 3 and the denominator has been multiplied by 4. In (D), the numerator has been multiplied by 4 and the denominator has been multiplied by a number less than 4.

17. D: The denominator has been multiplied by 3 to get 21. Think of what number multiplied by 3 totals 18.

18. C: Divide the numerator and denominator by 14.

19. A: Divide 68 by 7. The answer is 9 with a remainder of 5.

20. C: 10% of 900 are 90. Multiply 90 by 4 to find 40%.

21. A: Divide 3 by 60 to get .05 or 5%.

22. D: Divide 1 by 25 to get .04 or 4%.

23. D: Divide 4 by 16 (not 16 by 4).

24. D: To solve, first get both fractions on the same side of the equation to isolate the percentage sign. When $\frac{5}{6}$ is moved to the opposite side of the equation, it must be divided by the fraction there: $\frac{1}{3} \div \frac{5}{6}$ To divide one fraction into another, multiply by the reciprocal of the denominator: $\frac{1}{3} \times \frac{6}{5} = \frac{6}{15} = \frac{2}{5} = 40\%$.

25. D: To solve, divide 15 into 3.

26. D: To solve, first write the fraction as $\frac{8}{100}$.

Reduce by dividing numerator and denominator both by 4.

27. D: To solve change $2\frac{1}{2}\%$ to a decimal: .0250. Now add an x for the question mark:

$$.0250x = 6.25$$

Divide 6.25 by .0250.

28. D: To solve, rewrite the percent as a fraction: $\frac{30}{100}$. Then reduce the fraction.

29. C: To change a percent to a decimal, remove the percent sign and move the decimal two spaces to the left.

30. D: To solve, rewrite the equation with a decimal in place of the percent:

$12 = .25x$

$$x = \frac{12}{.25} = \frac{1200}{25} = 48$$

31. D: To solve, change the percent to a decimal:

$$.32x = 96$$

$$x = \frac{96}{.32} = \frac{9600}{32} = 300$$

32. A: To solve, add 6 a and 2a, then subtract 4a.

33. D: To solve, combine like terms, ensuring that the subtraction sign is notice and positive/negative signs are changed accordingly:

$$x^2 - x^2 = 0;\ -3x - 3x = 6x;\ -3 - 3 = -6$$

34. B: To solve, get the variable (y) by itself:

$$4x = 21\text{-}5;\ 4y = 16;\ y = 4$$

35. B: To solve, first do the multiplication on each side of the equation: $3x + 42 = 4x + 36$. Then get like terms on opposite sides of the equation: x = 6

36. B: Since they are like terms, just subtract. The result will be a negative number

37. B: To solve, first do the operations in parenthesis, then add like terms:

$$4x + 8 - 12 + 3x + 15 = 7x + 20$$

38. D: To solve, get like terms on opposite sides of the equation: $4x = 28;\ x = 7$

39. B: To solve, first do the operations in parenthesis, then add/subtract like terms in order to get like terms on opposite sides of the equation:

$$2r + 8 + 8 = 4r + 12$$

$$2r + 16 = 4r + 12;\ 4 = 2r;\ r = 2$$

40. C: It is quickest to find 20% of each answer given. (A): 10% of 80 is 8, so 20% is 16. (B): 10% of 160 is 16, so 20% is 32. (C): 10% of 200 is 20, so 20% is 40. (D): 10% of 800 is 80, so 20% is 160.

Applied Mathematics Answers

1. C: Use a proportion to solve the problem. 8/6 = x/15, 60 = 3x, x = 20.

2. D: (75 + 65 + 80 + 95 + 65)/5 = 76.

3. D: Gerald spends $50 on the "other" category. The percentage he spends on other as related to his entire food budget is 50/300, or approximately 16%.

4. C: To determine Gerald's annual food budget, multiply his monthly budget ($300) by 12 and get $3600.

5. A: Gerald spends $160 on produce, breads, and frozen food combined. This is more than $150 (half his food budget).

6. B: 10/50 = 20/100 = 20%.

- 103 -

7. C: 400/6 = 180/x, 400x = 1080, x = 2.7. Rounded to the nearest hour, it will take her approximately 3 hours.

8. D: x/3 + 4 = 7, x/3 = 3, x = 9.

29. C: $1\frac{1}{2}$ x 3 = $4\frac{1}{2}$.

10. B: Approximately $\frac{5}{7}$ of the year is non-weekend days. $365,000 x $\frac{5}{7}$ = $260,714.

11. C: (175 + 320 + 417 + 533 + 210)/5 = 331.

12. A: The income ($7,056,238) minus expenses ($3,998,100) = $3,058,138.

13. D: -10 is greater than -(-(-15)), which can also be written as -15.

14. A: -4 – (-9) = -4 + 9 = 5.

15. C: 184,770 divided by 12,318 is 15.

16. B: T + C = 21. T = 3C + 1. If you solve for 21 – C = 3C + 1, you get 3C + C = 20. 4C = 20. C = 5.

17. C: 0.09356 – 0.003784 is 0.089776.

18. C: 8/X = 40/100 = 2/5. 8 x 5 = 2X. 40 = 2X. x = 20.

19. B: A 20% increase in both sides gives dimensions of 24 and 36. To find the area, we multiply 24 x 36 and get 864 square inches.

20. C: (-4)(-2)(-6) = 8 x (-6) = -48.

21. A: Volume = LWH. Here that is 14 x 10 x 3 = 420.

22. D: 14/40 = X/100. 1400 = 40X. X = 35.

23. D: The number of students who received a C or a B is 22; the number of students who received a D or an F is 8. 22 – 8 = 14.

24. C: 2/10 = 1/5.

25. A: The equation for finding perimeter is P = 2L + 2W. Here P = 2x300 + 2x640 = 600 + 1280 = 1880.

26. B: 2^3 + (4 + 1) = 2 x 2 x 2 + 5 = 8 + 5 = 13.

27. C: The total amount of the bill is: 3.70/x = 8/100; 370 = 8x; x = $46.25.

28. B: If E + B = 225, and E = 2B + 5, then 225 – B = 2B + 5. Solving for B, 3B = 220 and B = 73.3. 225 – 73.3 = 151.7.

29. B: The average rate of cooling is: (86° - 38°) / 9 hrs; 48° / 9 = 5.33° F per hour.

30. D: Calculate the weighted average of the 3 tests: (80+75+92) / 3 = 82.3; Calculate the average of the 2 oral quizzes: (22/25) x 100 = 88 and (19/25) x 100 = 76, so (88 + 76)/2 = 82. Multiply each

grade by their weight, and then add them all up to determine the final grade: (82 x .45) + (88 x .25) + (91 x .15) + (82 x .15) = 85.

31. C: Calculate the average price as [(3.5 x 2) + (0.3 x 5) + (1.25 x 3) + (0.45 x 6)] / (2 + 5 + 3 + 6) = 0.93.

32. D: Remember the order of operations: (27 ÷ 9) = 3 and ($\sqrt{25}$ x 2) = 10; 3 x 10 = 30.

33. B: Double the number that is added to the previous number. So, 4+2=6, 6+4=10, 10+8=18, 18+16=34, and 34+32=66.

34. B: 144 x 0.40 = 57.6 + 144 = 201.6 and 168 x 0.40 = 67.2 + 168 = 235.2; then, convert to feet: 201.6/12 = 16.8 ft and 235.2/12 = 19.6 ft.

35. D: 1 gallon = 128 ounces, so 8 x 128 = 1,024 ounces for 8 gallons. 1/2 = 64 gallons, and 1/4= 32 gallons, so 64 + 32 = 96 ounces to fill the 3/4 gallons; the total ounces required is 1,024 + 96 = 1,120 ounces.

36. B: If mangoes are represented by x and coconuts are represented by y, then:

x + y = 10, and 2x + 4y = 30

2(10-y) + 4y = 30

20 – 2y + 4y = 30

2y = 10

y = 5 and x = 5, or 5 of each type of fruit

37. A: The average number of houses painted is: 5 + 9 + 15 + 20 + 25 / 5 =14.8 or 15.

38. B: Given the increasing trend, the data can be extrapolated from 25 to about 31, the closest possible answer.

39. D: 12(45 – 8) = 540 – 96 = 444, but 45(12 – 8) = 540 – 360 = 180.

40. A: Using the Pythagorean theorem: $25^2 + 35^2 = c^2$. 625 + 1225 = c^2. c =sqrt 1850 = 43.01.

41. A: Total number of students = 14 + 9 + 5 + 2 = 30. Total number of students with either green or hazel eyes: 5 + 2 = 7. To convert the fraction into a percentage: $\frac{7}{30} = \frac{x}{100}$. 700 = 30x. x = 23.3.

42. C: 14 brown + 9 blue = 23; 5 hazel + 2 green = 7; 23 (blue+brown)– 7 (hazel+green) = 16 more blue- or brown-eyed students than hazel- or green-eyed students.

43. D: Brown eyes = 14 and Green eyes = 2. So, the ratio of blue-eyed students to green-eyed students is 14:2 or 7:1.

44. A: $\frac{1}{2}$/ 15 = 4 3/5 / X; $\frac{1}{2}$X = 15 x 23/5. $\frac{1}{2}$X = 69. X = 69 x 2 = 138.

45. A: V = $\pi r^2 h$. V = 3.14 x (3^2) x 12. 3.14 x 9 x 12 = 339.12.

46. B: The equation for perimeter (P) = 2L + 2W. So, 600 = 2(250) + 2W. Solve for W: 600 – 500 = 2W. 100 = 2W. W = 50.

47. D: Multiplying a negative number by another negative number yields a positive

number, in this case -2 x -10 = +20, which is the largest answer choice.

48. C: (0.45 + 0.0 + 0.75 + 1.20 + 1.1 + 0.2 + 0.0) / 7 = 0.53.

49. C: He would have to pull out at least 9 (5 + 2 + 1 + 1) to make sure he has a yellow one.

50. B: He gets paid $12.00/hr for the first 40 hrs: 12 x 40 = $480. For time-and-a-half: 5 x 1.5 = 7.5.
7.5 x 12 = $90. So, 480 + 90 = $570.

Thank You

We at Mometrix would like to extend our heartfelt thanks to you, our friend and patron, for allowing us to play a part in your journey. It is a privilege to serve people from all walks of life who are unified in their commitment to building the best future they can for themselves.

The preparation you devote to these important testing milestones may be the most valuable educational opportunity you have for making a real difference in your life. We encourage you to put your heart into it—that feeling of succeeding, overcoming, and yes, conquering will be well worth the hours you've invested.

We want to hear your story, your struggles and your successes, and if you see any opportunities for us to improve our materials so we can help others even more effectively in the future, please share that with us as well. **The team at Mometrix would be absolutely thrilled to hear from you!** So please, send us an email (support@mometrix.com) and let's stay in touch.

If you feel as though you need additional help, please check out the other resources we offer:

Study Guide: http://MometrixStudyGuides.com/TABE

Flashcards: http://MometrixFlashcards.com/TABE